REVELATION UNRAVELED

Hidden Secrets of the Apocalypse

by
WILLIAM TAPLEY

©2007

THIRD EAGLE BOOKS
3038 Wall Street
Forestport, NY 13338

Tapley, William
Revelation Unraveled:
Hidden Secrets of the Apocalypse

ISBN-978-0-9798722-0-4

TABLE OF CONTENTS

REVELATION UNRAVELED

Hidden Secrets of the Apocalypse

Revelation Organized (

	1	2	3	4
W	6:1-2 *1st Seal* WHITE HORSE APOSTASY	6:9-11 5th Seal INNOCENT BLOOD	8:6-7 1st Trumpet HAIL, FIRE AND BLOOD	8:13 9:1-12 5th Trumpet STINGING LOCUSTS
R	6:3-4 2nd Seal RED HORSE WAR	6:12-17 6th Seal GOD'S WRATH	8:8-9 2nd Trumpet MOUNTAIN OF FIRE	9:13-21 6th Trumpet HUGE ARM'
B	6:5-6 3rd Seal BLACK HORSE FAMINE	7:1-17 Interlude SEALED TRIBES OF ISRAEL	8:10-11 3rd Trumpet WORM-WOOD	10:1-11 11:1-14 Interlude TWO PROPHETS
P	6:7-8 4th Seal PALE HORSE DEATH	8:1-5 7th Seal SILENCE IN HEAVEN	8:12 4th Trumpet DARKENED SUN	11:15-19 7th Trumpet EARTH-QUAKE AND HAIL

logically (ROC) Chart

5	6	7	8	9
12:1-6 EAT SIGN RED RAGON	14:6-7 1st Herald Angel GOSPEL PREACHED	15:1-8 16:1-2 1st Bowl GRIEVOUS WOUND	16:10-11 5th Bowl GOD BLASPHEMED	17:1-18 HARLOT ASTRIDE BEAST
2:7-18 OMAN FLEES RAGON	14:8 2nd Herald Angel "BABYLON IS FALLEN"	16:3 2nd Bowl BLOOD IN SEA	16:12 6th Bowl EUPHRATES DRIED UP	18:1-24 19:1-4 FALL OF BABYLON
3:1-18 TWO EASTS	14:9-13 3rd Herald Angel MARK OF THE BEAST	16:4-7 3rd Bowl RIVERS MADE BLOOD	16:13-16 Interlude ANTICHRIST GATHERS ARMY	19:5-16 CHRIST GATHERS ARMY
4:1-5 44,000 AVED RGINS	14:14-30 4th Herald Angel GRIM REAPER	16:8-9 4th Bowl SUN SCORCHES	16:17-21 7th Bowl GREAT CITY DIVIDED	19:17-21 20:1-15 FINAL VICTORY

UNRAVELING REVELATION

PROPHECY

The beautiful thing about true prophecy is that it never goes out of date. The not-so-beautiful part is that people rarely heed prophecy. This is why Jesus said, "A prophet is not without honor, except in his own country." (Mt. 13:57) Prophecy calls people to repentance, and that remains an unpopular message.

Today, many people disregard Our Lady's warnings to the shepherd children at Fatima, saying they are now obsolete. They will learn soon enough, too soon for many, the exact opposite is the truth. The Fatima prophecies become increasingly critical as we approach the end of days.

Much of what Mary predicted at Fatima has already proved accurate. Her predictions foretold the end of World War I, the outbreak of World War II, and the rise of Communism. Her warning that if Russia is not converted, "several entire nations will be annihilated" has yet to be fulfilled. People do not want to hear about their own possible destruction. Nowadays, few priests talk about the Fatima warnings from the pulpit. More was preached about Fatima forty years ago than is today. A rude awakening awaits the Church.

Many prophecies from the Old Testament are also pertinent to these last days and they verify that the Fatima message will come true for the present generation. For example, Ezechiel said that fire would rain down on Russia and America: "And I will send fire on Magog, and on them down that dwell confidently in the islands: and they shall know that I am the Lord." (Eze. 39:6) Most scripture interpreters believe that "Magog" is Russia and that "those who dwell confidently in the islands" refers to America.

The greatest prophet of all, of course, was Jesus our Messiah, the Son of God. One of the many signs He said to look for at the end of time is that it would be "as in the days of Sodom and Gomorrah." (Luke 17:29) Can anyone doubt that America and the West are becoming another Sodom and Gomorrah? Ezechiel's promise of "fire from the sky" may very well be imminent indeed!

In addition to nations living like Sodom and Gomorrah, Jesus said that at the time of the second coming of the Son of Man, "They will be as at the time of Noah, eating and drinking, marrying and giving in marriage, right up until the end." (Mt. 24:37-38) Is this a paradox since every species of animal on this planet must eat and reproduce in order to survive? But in fact, if man lives merely like the animals, and not by every word that comes forth from the mouth of God, he will not only not survive, he will destroy himself. Jesus said of His second coming, "If I do not come, there will be no flesh left on earth." (Mt. 24:22)

Another example of prophecy is King David dancing naked (or nearly so) in front of the Ark of the Covenant. Here David represents Jesus naked on the cross while the Ark of the Covenant is a symbol of His mother Mary. David's wife Micoh, who despises David's actions, represents the Jewish nation which will reject the sacrifice of Jesus their Messiah, while the servant girls, who appreciate David's performance, stand for the gentiles who will accept Christ's humiliation on the cross. God punishes Micoh for her tunnel vision and she becomes forever barren.

All true prophecy can be summed up in one sentence: "Repent, for the Kingdom of God is at hand." John the Baptist preached this to announce the coming of the Messiah. Although I am an interpreter of prophecy, and not a prophet myself, I can confidently, along with anyone else who wishes to, put on the mantle of a true prophet merely by shouting from the rooftops: "REPENT, AMERICA AND YOU WESTERN NATIONS — YOUR DAYS OF FREEDOM ARE AT AN END."

THE PROPHETIC BOOK OF ESTHER

Many other Old Testament events besides Sodom and Gomorrah and the Great Flood are prophetic as well as instructive. An extensive prophetic narrative is the Old Testament Book of Esther. Not just an inspiring epic of heroic conflict, the Book of Esther predicts the end times of both the Old and New Testaments. The actions and characters have direct counterparts in future events. Prophets of the Twentieth Century who describe "three days of darkness," a "great chastisement" and "secrets of heaven and earth" can find verification for such occurrences in the centuries old Book of Esther.

The story begins with a great feast hosted by Ahasuerus, a fifth century BC King of Persia, a party which lasts 180 days. At the end of the 180 days, Ahasuerus calls for an additional seven-day feast to which the common people are invited, not just the nobility. The crux of the story occurs when the King summons Vashti, his queen, to come with her crown and show her beauty to the assembled crowd. Vashti, however, can't be bothered. She has assembled a party of her own, comprised of women from the city, and she refuses his request. Not surprisingly, this angers Ahasuerus and his advisers remind him that unless Vashti is expelled as queen, women everywhere will likewise begin to snub their husbands. So the King exiles Vashti and eventually chooses the beautiful Jewish maiden Esther to take her place.

As is true with many Biblical stories, which may be looked back upon as allegorical, the personage of the King represents God. At one point Esther actually sees Ahasuerus, who quite probably is the historical Persian regent Xerxes, with the visage of an angel. As the beautiful Jewish queen, Esther undoubtedly represents the Blessed Virgin Mary.

Vashti, on the other hand, symbolizes the Old Testament Jews who refuse to share their "beauty" (the one true revealed religion) at the appropriate time in history with the common people (gentiles). It's interesting to note that King Ahasuerus does not execute Vashti, as Henry the Eighth might have done, but banishes her instead, just as God did not destroy the Jewish religion, even after the Catholic Church became His new bride, His new Chosen People.

At this point, the Book of Esther shifts from its veiled predictions about the end of the Old Testament to hidden prophecies about an event even further into the future, the end of the New Testament! Esther and her people must confront a terrible enemy, Haman, who is a figure of the Antichrist. Both Haman and the Antichrist seek to destroy God's Chosen People. For Haman it's the Jews, for the Antichrist, it is the Catholic Christians.

Haman, who serves as the King's prime minister, particularly hates the Jew, Mordecai, who refuses to pay Haman any kind of homage. Unbeknownst to Haman, Mordecai is Queen Esther's uncle. By not respecting Haman and by striving mightily to save his people from Haman's evil schemes, Mordecai prefigures a great Pope of the end times, quite possibly the last Pope predicted by St. Malachy, called Pope Peter II.

If Mordecai stands for a Pope, the many eunuchs in the Book of Esther foreshadow the celibate priesthood of the Roman Catholic Church. But, like today's clergy, not all the eunuchs are trustworthy.

Two of the eunuchs are assassins who attempt to overthrow King Ahasuerus in a plot which is thwarted by Mordecai (another reason Haman hates Mordecai). This should give hope to present day Catholics that an end time Pope, possibly Benedict XVI or Peter II[1], will excommunicate apostate priests, bishops and cardinals.

The good eunuchs help prepare Esther so that her appearance will impress the King. These eunuchs foreshadow faithful end times clergy and religious who are supportive of the Church and the Papacy. In Revelation, St. John prophesies there will be 144,000 "virgins" who are faithful enough to be raptured and will reign with Christ during the Millennium. (14:1-4)

Haman's evil scheme is to effect the murder of all Jews throughout Persia on the thirteenth day of the month of Adar, the last month of the year. Mordecai hears of these plans and begs Esther to intercede with the King who is swayed by her appeals and abruptly turns the tables on Haman. Thus, at the last minute, the Jews, in a sudden and complete reversal of fortune, snatch victory from the jaws of defeat on the fifteenth day of Adar.

Haman and his ten sons are hanged on the same gibbet planned for Mordecai, just as the Antichrist and his ten kings, as described in Revelation, will be defeated at the last minute and thrust into the lake of fire. This victory over Haman, although not its future significance, is celebrated to this day by Jews throughout the world as the feast of Purim. "Purim" means "lots" because Haman chose the thirteenth day to exterminate the Jews by casting lots.

Two important lessons emerge from the prophetic aspects of the Book of Esther for those of us living in these last days and months of the New Testament. First, our victory over the Antichrist will occur only at the last moment, just when everything seems hopeless, and second, it will be accomplished by a Pope pleading on behalf of his people to the Blessed Mother to intercede with God our Father. This may take the form of a clear and forthright consecration of Russia to the Immaculate Heart of Mary as called for decades ago by the Blessed Mother herself to Sister Lucia of Fatima.[2] If the consecration is not carried out, Mary may effect victory by bringing upon us the chastising comet which will

---

[1]According to St. Malachy's prophecies, the last two Popes are Benedict XVI and Peter II. However, St. Malachy may have left off his list false popes or antipopes who may come in between or occur simultaneously with these last two popes.
[2]In 1984, Pope John Paul II consecrated the "world" to the Immaculate Heart of Mary but since he did not mention "Russia" by name, he added the words: "Enlighten especially those peoples of which you await our consecration." Many people believe the Pope added this disclaimer because he himself adjudged the consecration to be insufficient.

wipe out the end-times One World Tyranny of the Antichrist and the One World Religion of the False Prophet.

By examining the preponderance of significant numbers in the Book of Esther, we find many verifications that this is indeed a prophetic text. King Ahasuerus' great party lasts 180 days which is a half-year and symbolizes the time frame of the Old Testament, or, in other words, the first half of revealed scripture. The following short seven-day party, to which even the common people are invited, represents the short public ministry of Jesus to the gentiles as well as the Jews, and thus foretells the separating period between the Old and New Testaments. The Chosen People sadly reject their Messiah, just as Vashti rejects her king.

Many numbers which occur in the second part of Esther are also important in identifying its end-time character. That Esther's struggle with Haman occurs during Adar, the last month of the year, shows that we are talking symbolically about a final battle. Mordecai's dream sequence about two "dragons" raging war, which is told about in the Greek version of Esther, is obviously Apocalyptic in nature.

The start of the battle on the thirteenth day reflects the Fatima appearances of our Blessed Mother which always occurred on the thirteenth day of the month. The thirteenth day of Adar, along with the two ensuing days, signify the three days of darkness. The day of final victory on the fifteenth of Adar points to the fifteen decades of the rosary as the primary weapon which defeats the Antichrist. (Incidentally, this may be an indication that adding five decades to the rosary is a possible danger which lessens the numerical impact of the original fifteen decades as revealed to St. Dominick by the Blessed Mother. However, we will also see later on that the new Luminous Mysteries are significant in analyzing Revelation.)

Another way to show that fifteen is an essential number in defeating the Antichrist is to investigate fractional equivalents. Six Six Six, the number of the beast, can be expressed as a decimal .666 which is the fraction 2/3. When man (the number two represents mankind, a man and a woman) places himself before God or over God (three represents the Trinity), you obtain the most evil number of all. Even the Hollywood movie *The Number* 23 showed the Satanic evil of placing man before God. Conversely, three before or over two (3/2) indicates the proper relationship — God's superiority over man. The resulting decimal is 1.5 and, after eliminating the decimal point, as also done with .666, we get 15. Fifteen can be expressed as 555 for the Joyful, Sorrowful, and Glorious Mysteries of the rosary. Both evil numbers 666 and 444 (2/3 x 2/3) must be forever subservient to the very powerful number 555!

The end times importance of the number five is also indicated by the five smooth pebbles that young David chooses to slay Goliath (who, like Haman, is a symbolic forerunner of the Antichrist) (1 Kings 17:40). David really needs only one pebble, but by taking five smooth pebbles, clearly rosary imagery, he is predicting that Christ's defeat of the Antichrist will come about through Mary.

Another important event which indicates that the Book of Esther is prophetic is Mordecai's dream sequence. Mordecai sees a great battle between two dragons, all the nations are involved, but then a little fountain grows into a great river, and ultimately the sun rises and the humble are exalted. It's not hard to understand that this is an apocalyptic vision.

Mordecai's Dream
from the Book of Esther

11:5   And this was his dream: Behold there were voices, and tumults, and thunders, and a great disturbance upon earth.

11:6   And behold two great dragons came forth ready to fight one against another.

11:7   And at their cry all nations were stirred up to fight against the nation of the just.

11:8   And that was a day of darkness and danger, of tribulation and distress and great fear upon earth.

11:9   And the nation of the just was troubled fearing their own evils, and was prepared for death.

11:10   And they cried to God: and as they were crying, a little fountain grew into a very great river, and abounded into many waters.

11:11   The light and the sun rose up, and the humble were exalted, and they devoured the glorious.

Mordecai's interpretation of his dream can easily be updated for an end-times application. The two dragons symbolize the last great pope, Peter II and either the False Pope or the Antichrist. "All the nations" are the same as those in the Apocalypse which have "one purpose" (Rev. 17:13) which is to destroy the Catholic Church. The "day of darkness" refers to Armagedon and the "little fountain" which grows into a very great river is the Blessed Virgin Mary. The victory at the end shows that the saints will eventually triumph over the forces of the Antichrist and will reign a thousand years with Him during the Millennium.

The Book of Esther, which comes near the middle of the Old Testament, reminds us of God's promise at the very beginning of the

Bible (Genesis) that the Woman (Mary) and her seed (spiritual children) would crush the head of Satan, and that this will be fully accomplished at the Apocalyptic very end of the Bible.

ORIGINAL SIN

Mary's role in crushing the head of Satan was precipitated by Adam and Eve's fall from grace in the Garden of Eden. Some claim that since Eve sinned first, women must be inferior creatures and God would never give such an exalted role to Mary. But, if you find it difficult to see Mary's crucial role in these end times, you will find it even more difficult to accept my claim that women are, sad to say, morally superior to men.

How often have we heard, for example, that women cannot be Roman Catholic priests because they are inferior to men? I say this is a complete falsehood. Well, not completely, because it's true that women cannot be priests (or heads of households for that matter). But the reason is not because women are inferior. It's rather because they are in fact morally superior. In this chapter, I will attempt to explain this contradiction.

If women are in fact superior, is there a decisive way, that is, a Biblical way, to prove it? Certainly in the beginning, man and woman, meaning Adam and Eve, were created equal. Neither Adam nor Eve had any superiority over the other. When God first shows Eve to Adam, he exclaims, "At last, flesh of my flesh and bone of my bone!" (Genesis 3:23) This can only connote absolute equality.

Even those who disagree with my premise that women are superior must admit that the equality which existed between the sexes at creation is no longer in force. Most Christians would immediately recognize that the problem is original sin. But if women are morally superior to men, that can only mean that the original sin of woman (that is, Eve's sin) must not have been as serious as Adam's. If this is true, wouldn't women make better priests? (Of course, if there were no original sin, there would be no need for priests!)

The reason Adam's original sin was worse than Eve's is because he succumbed to the temptations from his wife, that is, another human being. Eve, on the other hand, succumbed to the wiles of Satan himself, a supernatural creature. Eve therefore had more excuse to fail. Accordingly, many claim that if Adam had not fallen, there would have been no original sin whatsoever. It is Adam's greater guilt that makes him, and men in general, morally inferior to Eve and all women. (A priest friend of mine disagrees with me and says, "I hear women's confessions.")

Some may claim men are superior because when God came to earth and took on human flesh, he came as the man Jesus Christ. God could have been incarnated as a woman but scripture says, "He humbled Himself and became man." If He could have humbled Himself more by becoming a woman, He would have! But He humbled Himself to the max by adopting the lowest form of humanity, manhood.

If all this is true, isn't it obvious that a clear case could be made for women to be priests? No, because, although women are morally superior, they still are tainted by original sin and are not perfect. To avoid the sin of Eve, women must do the opposite of Eve. Her sin was one of pride, succumbing to the serpent's promise of achieving wisdom, of knowing good and evil and therefore becoming like God. Women's hope in perfecting themselves now means that they must humble themselves, thereby reversing Eve's original sin of pride. Adam's sin was of putting the woman before God and not resisting Eve's suggestions. To correct Adam's sin of acquiescence to evil, man now must assert his authority and lead himself and the woman back to God's standard.

It is very tempting for Catholic Bishops to resolve the shortage of priests by advocating women priests. This plan will fail just as it has in other Christian denominations where it has been tried. The men simply stop going to church. Then you have no shortage of priestesses, but a shortage of congregation. Even in Catholic parishes where the first step has been taken in this direction with the introduction of altar girls, the would-be altar boys soon quit and the result is one priest surrounded by female lectors, female eucharistic ministers, and female altar servers. Since most priestly vocations in the past came from the ranks of altar boys, replacing altar boys with girls merely exacerbates the shortage of priests.

Men, like Adam, are more than willing to let women take over, but in doing so, they abdicate their responsibility to assert authority and be the moral leaders of mankind, thereby reversing the sin of Adam. Woman chafe at being in a "lower" social position and are eager to show off their "higher" moral knowledge, but by not being humble, they are not reversing the sin of Eve and instead are perpetuating it.

So why do men lessen their church attendance when morally superior women are allowed behind the pulpit? Because the man says, "I cannot be as good as she is," and walks out. Thus weak-willed Bishops who advocate women priests are repeating the sin of Adam by not exercising their authority, while feminist nuns who want to be priests are repeating Eve's sin of pride. They ignore God's dictum to Eve that because of her original sin, "You will be under your husband's power and he shall have dominion over you." (Gen. 3:16)

AFTER THE FALL

The same proper relationship between men and women should prevail not only in the Catholic priesthood and in Catholic marriage, but also during Catholic courtship. A good example can be found in the Old Testament Book of Tobias. The young woman Sarah has been married seven times but each husband has died on their wedding night because she is afflicted by a demon "Asmodeus" and her husbands wanted to marry her for the sake of lust and not to have children.

Tobias, with the guidance of the Archangel Raphael, convinces Sarah's family that his marriage to her, unlike her seven previous attempts, will succeed. On their wedding night, Tobias tells Sarah they must refrain from intimacy for three nights and, in order to overpower Asmodeus, he will burn the liver of a fish in their wedding chamber (following the instructions of Raphael). What important lessons can we learn from this story?

Today, many young women, Catholics included, don't wish to refrain from intimacy weeks and even months before the marriage ceremony, let alone for three days afterwards! Here is where the young Catholic and Christian man must learn from Adam's mistake, oppose his fiancee's weakness, and steer her in the right direction. If perhaps her weakness is alcohol, the worldly man will take advantage of the situation and try to get her drunk. The good man of integrity will see the problem and stay clear of bars or parties where alcohol is served. Perhaps her problem is drugs. Again, the good man will help her away from temptation.

A common problem for young people today seems to be perverse sex. Now, if a young female White House intern happens to be afflicted by this particular Asmodeus, and you are a totally amoral United States president, you take advantage of her. But a true, morally upright man will not take the easy way, the wide path to Hell. He must direct his Sarah onto the narrow path. Of course, the young woman may not want her demon exorcised, and the moral man may endure a lengthy search for his right Sarah, but when he finds her, she will follow his high moral leadership.

And so, young women, look to Sarah for your model. You may think you know better and this writer will admit you are morally superior, but you must also admit you are not perfect yet. If your intended wants to follow church teaching and refrain from intimacy before marriage, it is your duty to obey. Even if he wants to do something that may seem a little flakey — after all, burning a fish liver in your honeymoon bedroom is not exactly incense — remember Sarah obeyed Tobias and scripture states they had a happy marriage and lived to see their children's children.

None of us can go back to the Garden of Eden. People who go to nudist camps make a sad attempt but can only fail. Nor can we ever claim that men and women will somehow regain equality. When we deny original sin and its societal effects, we are really denying that we need Jesus as our Messiah. The church needs priests and nuns just as married men and women need each other. We can all attain perfection, both men and women, even as our heavenly Father is perfect, by practicing humility. For woman, humility is realizing that she can never have authority over man. For man, it is understanding that despite his moral inferiority to a woman, he has a responsibility to assume leadership in both the family and the church.

To those who might claim that the Catholic Church discriminates against women, I say the facts are otherwise. In Washington, DC, for instance, the hallways of government are lined with bronze busts of famous American officials in history. Approximately ninety-five percent are male. If you check out the annual reports of leaders in American industry, ninety percent of CEOs are men.

If your daughter wants equal opportunity in government or industry, her chances are slim. But if she is willing to be a saint of the Catholic Church, fully fifty percent of canonized saints are women. If you want to cast stones about inequality between the sexes, it is absurd to start with the Catholic Church.

The two most famous Catholics in the Twentieth Century were Pope John Paul II and Mother Teresa. I've noticed recently that some in the entertainment industry are beginning to disparage even Mother Teresa. That's because Hollywood despises those of faith, preferring to adulate "bimbos."

So, young women, if you want both success and respect, forget the Hollywood ideal and practice your Faith. In these latter days, both men and women must look to "Mary and her seed (spiritual children)" if any of us expect to fulfill our destiny and crush the head of the serpent as promised in Gen. 3:15.

THE TRINITARIAN NATURE OF GOD
AND HIS UNIVERSE

Before studying the Apocalypse (Revelation), it's important that we understand the three divine persons in one God, who we know as the Father, Son, and Holy Spirit, and how that truth is expressed in the threefold or trinitarian nature of the universe. As every student learns, there are three states of matter, three primary colors, three primary shapes, etc. It will be amazing to discover how the numerous trinities in nature express the individual character of each person of the Godhead. It's as if God were a great artist who signed His name on His masterpiece in triplicate.

Clues to the character of each person in the Trinity may be found in their family names. God the Father expresses strength or stability, just like the father in a family. His son Jesus, like any youth, expresses vitality. And lastly, the Holy Spirit represents the mother in a family and therefore the mystery of the feminine. This does not mean that the Holy Spirit Himself is feminine, but rather He is the Lord of procreation, the Lord and giver of life.

The universe itself in its entirety, most scientists agree, consists of the triad: time, space, and matter. I think it's appropriate that we consider each of these very different concepts as a reflection of each of the three divine persons. For example, of the three, matter is the most solid and thus represents the strength and stability of God the Father. Time can also be measured as motion and therefore represents the youthful nature of God the Son. Finally, the mystery of space reflects the feminine mystery of God the Holy Spirit. Thus, like the three persons of the Trinity, the three structural divisions of the universe are completely unique while at the same time totally unified.

Like many other trinities in nature, the three divides of the universe can be further broken down into additional trinities. Time consists of past, present and future. Space is expressed as horizontal (length), vertical (width) and front to back (depth). The three states of matter are solid, liquid, and gas. If we take a closer look at each of these sub-trinities, like the parts of the universe they are derived from, they very accurately reflect the individual natures of the Divine Trinity.

Regarding the universal phenomenon of time, the future is certainly the most mysterious and is easily understood as a reflection of the Holy Spirit. The present is the active aspect of time and expresses the energy and vitality of God the Son. Since the past is a known quantity, it reflects the stable nature of God the Father. Thus, although time itself, as one of the trinitarian aspects of the universe, reflects primarily the Son, when broken down into its three parts, it reflects all three persons of the Godhead.

The same kind of analysis can be applied to space. Horizontality expresses calmness, strength and serenity and therefore best reflects the Father. Verticality is a sign of activity, the lightning strike between heaven and earth, and thus reveals to us the Son. The front to back dimension of space is mysterious and therefore of the Holy

Spirit, because it is actually hidden from view and cannot be seen.

In similar comparisons, matter can be solid, like the Father, in motion or liquid, like the Son, or an unseen and mysterious gas, like the Holy Spirit. These three states of matter are also found in the three basic environments of our planet — land, sea, and air. Even the symbols that we associate with each person of the trinity — the fish for Jesus, the dove for the Holy Spirit, and, to a lesser degree, the ox for God the Father — are derived from their individual relationship with the three states of matter. Later on in our study of the Apocalypse, we will find a corresponding unholy trinity of Satan, the Antichrist and the False Prophet.

Other important trinities which are inherent in the structure of the universe include the three primary colors and the three primary shapes. All the myriad shades of pigment available to an artist can be mixed from just three colors: red, blue and yellow. Red, being the most vibrant and exciting of colors, bears the imprint of God the Son. Since blue is always considered cool, calm and collected, how better to describe God the Father? Yellow, like the gaseous flame of a candle, provokes an image of the Holy Spirit. One of the attractions of burning a candle to symbolize prayer is because the three parts thereof — the cool solid wax, the melted liquid, and the hot flame — combine to invoke the Trinity.

Just as all colors can be obtained from red, blue, and yellow, all forms in the universe can be derived from just three primary shapes: square, circle, and triangle. The square, clearly the most solid of these forms, reflects the Father. Because the line of a circle has no beginning or end, a circle reveals the Spirit as it is the most feminine and mysterious. The triangle also exhibits solidity but not as much as a square, especially if it is depicted resting on one of its points, and therefore signifies the more active qualities of the Son.

As we are discovering, it should not be surprising that the three primary shapes can also be further broken down into trinities. For example, there are three types of triangles: equilateral, scalene, and isosceles. Because all sides of an equilateral triangle are the same size, that sameness reflects stability and thus God the Father. Since all sides of a scalene triangle are different lengths, that variety reflects vitality and thus God the Son. The isosceles triangle is quite unusual because the two equal sides represent that which God the Father and Son have in common, their masculine traits, while the third length is different because it reflects the more feminine nature of God the Holy Spirit.

The three types of circular forms are the circle, ellipse, and heart. The circle, being the more basic and regular of these three shapes, reflects the Father. Tilting a circle causes it to become more obscure, more mysterious and more feminine in appearance and the resulting ellipse is thus more like the Holy Spirit. If you tilt and also bend a circle in half, the result is a heart shape. It's not too far afield that a heart shape should represent Jesus. When a priest breaks in half the consecrated host (circle), the symbolism of sacrifice and a broken heart is complete. We read in Luke 24:13 that several disciples did not recognize the risen Jesus until the "breaking of the bread." Like the bread and the heart, Jesus was broken on the cross.

Another important trinity is the sun, moon, and stars. Jesus says that the end times would be marked by signs in the sun, moon and stars (Mt. 24:30). Contrary to popular belief, the sun does not symbolize the Son, but rather God the Father. The moon, on the other hand, reflects the sun, just as Jesus reflects the Father. Also, the moon's changing appearance every night further establishes it as a symbol of the active nature of the Son. The stars, many so tiny as to be invisible, are part of deep and mysterious space, and therefore a representation of the Spirit.

All the above are examples of what I term "structural" trinities because they are at the core of the inherent foundation of the universe. The more I study trinities, the more I realize there are a plethora of trinities, even within trinities, and yes, there are three kinds of trinities.

If the structural trinities represent God the Father, a different type of trinity must represent God the Son. I call this new set the "gradation" trinities. A good example is the trio, small, medium and large. Since small is feminine, it describes the Holy Spirit, and, of course, large is masculine and thus representative of the Father. Medium can be a very wide range of sizes and thus exhibits the vitality of the Son.

Some of the trinities already discussed can be viewed as gradation trinities. The states of matter go from hot to cold. Ice is solid at 32° Fahrenheit and becomes a gas at 212° Fahrenheit. But there is a whole range of temperatures that water can exist at from very cold to very hot. Since gradation trinities show the character of God the Son, the emphasis is always on the variety of these middle ranges.

Other gradation trinities include smooth to rough, quiet to loud, soft to hard, slow to fast, short to tall, high pitch to low pitch, etc. In each case one extreme is feminine in nature, the other extreme is masculine while God the Son occupies the middle area. In fact, the entire life of Jesus, the Son of God on earth, depicts this gradual change. First He comes into earthly existence as a tiny, tender infant and eventually grows into manhood. One of the reasons our perverted society seems to accept abortion is because it fails to value smallness.

However, a tiny baby in his mother's womb, even if merely one fertilized cell, is a more exquisite and perfect image of the Holy Spirit, and a greater miracle of procreation than a full-grown adult.

Procreation is the dominant characteristic of the Holy Spirit and the primary feature which distinguishes Him from God the Father and Son. Therefore, the trinities associated with the third Person of the Trinity are called the "reproductive" trinities. The human family can be an example of a reproductive trinity. The aforementioned isosceles triangle is a reproductive trinity because two sides are the same length and one side different. The primary shapes can also be viewed as a reproductive trinity since the square and triangle are similar in appearance (each has sharp corners and straight sides) whereas a circle looks much different. Likewise, a man's body is square and angular while a woman is more rounded.

The reason I will never declare the Holy Spirit to be female is that while a woman's body very accurately reflects the Third Person, the Holy Spirit Himself is much more than just feminine. For instance, all the Holy Spirit characteristics, such as smallness, softness, and roundness, are also found in babies, both male and female. Even the male private parts could be described as a reproductive trinity and exhibit most other characteristics of the Holy Spirit, yet no one would call them "feminine." In fact, it's possible to go too far in trying to get a complete description of the Holy Spirit because His chief defining trait is mystery. And, isn't it true, a woman always likes to keep a man guessing?

When Jesus says, "He who see Me sees the Father," He indicates that He and the Father are, at least visually, very identical. Jesus does not say, "He who sees Me sees the Holy Spirit," because He and the Spirit look very different. But when Jesus speaks in abstract terms, "I am the Alpha and the Omega, the first and the last, the beginning and the end," (Rev. 22:14) then He is indeed saying, I am the Father (the Alpha or the First) and I am the Holy Spirit (the Omega or Last).

We find in scripture that God the Father is most associated with the Old Testament, that is, the past, while the Church of today and the future is guided by the Holy Spirit. God is "the one who is, who was, and who is to come." (Rev. 1:4) That's why in the human species, Adam, the male, who represents the Father, was created first and Eve, the female, who represents the Holy Spirit, was created last. Also, remember that Jesus' first miracle was changing water into wine, a miracle of matter and therefore of the Father, and Jesus' last miracle was changing wine into His blood, a miracle of the Spirit.

To summarize this chapter, mankind can perhaps begin to better understand the hidden mysteries of the Divine Trinity — Father, Son, and Holy Spirit — by examining the many wonderful trinities found in His creation. Without a doubt, there are countless trinities not examined here, such as melody, harmony and rhythm, faith, hope and charity, or even knife, fork, and spoon, but remember, it is impossible to pigeonhole God or to ever totally understand Him. However, if Saint Patrick could explain the Trinity by means of a simple shamrock, perhaps these short dissertations can carry the great Saint's comparisons just that much further.

PURPOSE OF PROPHECY

The third part of the book of Revelation (also called the Apocalypse) contains prophecies concerning the end times or, as the author St. John says, "The things which must come to pass hereafter." (4:1) Beginning with chapter six and continuing through chapter twenty, fifteen chapters inclusive, St. John describes many terrifying trials for mankind and for Christians in particular before Christ establishes a "new heaven and a new earth." (21:1)

These fifteen chapters are completely different from the other chapters of Revelation. The first three chapters contain letters from St. John written to seven churches in Asia: Ephesus, Smyrna, Pergamum, Thyatira, Sardis, Philadelphia, and Laodicea. These letters are all straightforward accounts, without any mysterious allegory or symbolism. No exegete ever bothers to analyze them in any way, other than how they are expressed, except to say that the churches no longer exist. If Revelation as a whole is a warning to the faithful, the disappearance of these Christian communities should remind us that our visible church will also cease to exist. In my own Catholic diocese (Syracuse, New York), already one-third of the churches are closing. During the reign of the Antichrist, all remaining places of worship will close or apostatize.

The fourth and fifth chapters introduce the reader to a different type of presentation which is mysterious, puzzling and full of symbolism. First, there is the mystery of four creatures with six wings who worship before the throne of God. This can be explained, if an explanation is possible, because heaven, like other events in the future about to be described, is inherently mysterious.

Next, we are introduced to the "Lamb" who stands for Jesus our Messiah, although the name "Jesus" is never mentioned. Instead the Lord is depicted as, "The horn of the Tribe of Judah", "the Root of David", the "Lamb that was slain", and "the Redeemer". He is also expressed by various adjectives and attributes, such as "worthy", "power", "divinity", "wisdom", "strength", "honor", "glory", and "benediction". It is becoming evident that the Book of the Apocalypse is really a poem and one explanation for all this mystery and symbolism is that these are devices a great poet always employs.

Until now, however, Revelation has remained largely hidden for several more important reasons. First, as other authors have noted, the events described could apply to many past trials and tribulations. Since Christianity and paganism can never coexist, previous skirmishes were but previews of the final battle. As in the Book of Esther, the struggle between good and evil is always relevant especially for the Old Testament Jews, but also increasingly relevant in these end days. All true prophecy becomes more relevant as time goes by.

Second, until only very recently, people could not comprehend how specific calamities such as ICBMs, nuclear war, 200 million-man armies, etc., might possibly occur. Therefore, St. John wrote about these woes in mysterious terms which could be unraveled only at the appropriate time. That time is now!

Third, the purpose of prophecy is not to establish that the prophet can see into the future. Prophecy is a warning from God that He intends to punish people, in what form this chastisement will take, why He is punishing and how to avoid it. This last salvific gift from God is the most important purpose of prophecy.

When Jonah warned the city of Nineveh of its imminent destruction, the whole city repented from king to slave and even the animals were clothed in sackcloth. God relented and Nineveh was spared. Prophecy is successful when the prophesied calamities are prevented.

Sometimes good people are called not to repent in order to avoid chastisement, but to escape instead. Noah built an ark to survive the great flood. Lot and his family were led safely out of Sodom and Gomorrah. And Jesus warned that before the Romans destroyed Jerusalem, Christians should read the signs and escape to the hills.

The Book of Revelation is no different except that the destruction will be the greatest chastisement God will ever mete out to the world. As Jesus said, the end times will be worse than men have ever seen before or will see again (Mt. 14:21). Obviously it is important that we know when the time is ripe and what we must do to escape. These fifteen end-time chapters, which provide the answers, were never meant to always remain a secret. For those of us living in this last generation, now is the time predestined for their unraveling!

RESTRUCTURING THE TEXT

For centuries, nearly 2000 years in fact, Popes, prelates, priests and Protestants, have tried to figure out the Book of Revelation. Why has it been so difficult? How can there be so many different interpretations? The problem is that in most cases these exegetes look at the unusual sequence of events and still maintain that St. John tells his story in chronological order. Even when analysts understand that the author relates the same events four or five times over, they still consider that at least the seven seals, trumpets and bowls are in the correct sequence. It will come as a great surprise to many that the fifteen end-times chapters must be totally restructured in order to uncover their hidden secrets because St. John organized them as a cryptogram!

Like the end-times prophecies, which are shrouded within its pages, Revelation exhibits a surface order and a hidden order. The surface order is based on the number seven: seven seals, seven trumpets, and seven bowls. Seven is the "perfect" number and has resonated with humanity ever since God gave Adam and Eve the seven day week.

Hidden under the surface organization of seven, the fifteen end-time chapters of the Apocalypse are actually structured around the number four. For each sequence of sevenfold events (seven seals, seven trumpets, seven bowls, etc.), St. John describes one additional unnumbered event placed between the sixth and seventh event, which adds up to a total of eight separate occurrences. This makes it possible to break these eight down into two equal groups of four which basically repeat each other. These four are separated again by a connecting section which we will see later describes the four mysteries of the Rosary, Joyful, Luminous, Sorrowful and Glorious. Thus the four horsemen of the Apocalypse divide the fifteen end-time chapters into four, not seven major subdivisions, which are separated again nine times for a total of thirty-six individual segments.

Because of this underlying fourfold structure, I have rearranged the text so that the nine sections headed by each of the four horsemen are placed in their approximately correct chronological order. For example, the nine events which pertain to the Great Apostasy (the Fifth Seal, 1st Trumpet, 5th Trumpet, Great Sign, 1st Herald Angel, 1st Bowl, 5th Bowl and Harlot Astride Beast) follow the first horseman, the White Horse. This makes it much easier to understand the symbolism. Thus when fire falls from heaven, a fairly common occurrence in the Apocalypse, the meaning is easier to extract when we know if it occurs during a physical or spiritual chastisement.

A good way to understand the new time sequence in the Apocalypse is to place the events on a chart like a calendar. (See REVELATION ORGANIZED CHRONOLOGICALLY [ROC] CHART.)

- **Far left column** lists the first Four Seals: the four horsemen. These are denoted by W for White Horse, R for Red Horse, B for Black Horse, and P for Pale Horse.
- **Second column:** the rest of the Seals, including the interlude between the Sixth and Seventh seals.
- **Third column:** the first four Trumpets
- **Fourth column:** Fifth Trumpet through the Seventh Trumpet, including the interlude between the Sixth and Seventh trumpets
- **Fifth column:** Great Sign, Woman Flees Dragon, Two Beasts, 144,000 Saved Virgins
- **Sixth column:** the four Herald Angels
- **Seventh column:** the first four Bowls
- **Eighth column:** Fifth Bowl through the Seventh Bowl, including the interlude between the Sixth and Seventh Bowl
- **Ninth column:** Harlot Astride Beast, Fall of Babylon, Christ Gathers Army, and the Final Victory.

If you follow the columns vertically, you will read the Apocalypse as it is found in your Bibles. But if you read the columns horizontally, like the days of the weeks on a calendar, the sequence following "W" (White Horse) reads "1st Seal, 5th Seal, 1st Trumpet, 5th Trumpet, Great Sign, 1st Herald Angel, 1st Bowl, 5th Bowl and Harlot Astride Beast." This makes for a more accurate chronological sequence and thus unlocks many of the hidden mysteries. If you read across the horizontal column following "R" (Red Horse War), you find "God's Wrath, Mountain of Fire, Huge Army, Woman Flees Dragon, 'Babylon is Fallen', Blood in the Sea, Euphrates Dried Up and Fall of Babylon." All these events happen during World War III when Communism (the scarlet Beast) obliterates Capitalism (the scarlet whore).

If we examine the aforementioned "common occurrence" of fire falling from heaven, when St. John describes a fiery object falling from the sky during the Apostasy, it very likely represents a fall from grace, in this instance, Martin Luther. If it falls during the last great war, WWIII, it is undoubtedly a physical chastisement, in this case an ICBM.

During the reign of the Antichrist, it would be Wormwood, who is the False Prophet, and during God's final judgment, it would again be a physical punishment, most likely meteorites from the chastising comet. It really helps in identifying the author's symbology to know its context. If the context doesn't automatically reveal the real meaning of an event, at least the ROC chart serves to exclude a lot of possibilities.

One way to realize that the original text is not in chronological order is to look at the single most important event in the Apocalypse, the fall of Babylon (Capitalism), which occurs in Chapters 17 and 18. In 17:1, an angel says, "Come, I will show you the condemnation of the great harlot." Yet an angel declares back in Chapter 14 that "great Babylon is fallen, is fallen" which is in the past tense. Also, in Chapter 16, St. John states, "And great Babylon came in remembrance before God." Again, Babylon's destruction is "remembered" before it takes place. When we reorder these passages according to the ROC chart, they all occur after the correct general heading of the second horseman, the Red Horse (War).

A further hint that rearranging the original text sequence will be beneficial is that the Beast from the abyss, the One World Tyranny (Socialist/Communism), makes its first appearance in Chapters 15 and 16 **after** this same Beast from the abyss makes war against the Two Witnesses and kills them in Chapter 11. Chapter 11's description of the activities of the Two Witnesses should be moved forward to the third major subdivision of the Apocalypse following the Black Horse, "Famine," during the Great Tribulation.

Still another way to appreciate the ROC chart is to look at the three woes. In St. John's original arrangement, the three woes are announced by the 5th, 6th and 7th Trumpet Angels. This means that all three woes occur within a space of three chapters — 9, 10, and 11. If the woes are significant, why are they not mentioned at all in 12 other chapters (6, 7, 8, and 12 - 20)?

With the new ROC arrangement, the woes occur during the tenures of all four horsemen. We find the first woe, the splitting up of Christianity, in section W-4. The second woe begins, not with the 6th trumpet, but with the 2nd trumpet at the start of World War III. This woe extends through the entire war cycle all the way through the first part of the tribulation until the point where the Two Witnesses are killed by the Beast from the abyss. The third woe begins with the 4th, not the 7th trumpet, and coincides with the Great Chastisement. The end of the third woe is never indicated in the original, but is assumed to be at the end of Chapter 11. It seems more plausible that it extends to the very end, Armagedon.

Other examples which support restructuring are the many paired events which only become apparent on the ROC chart. The two Beasts (B-5) directly follow the Two Witnesses (B-4). Christ gathers His army (B-9) immediately after the Antichrist gathers his forces (B-8). The land war (R-4) follows the air and sea battle (R-3). The pains and wounds on the seat (throne) of the Beast (W-9) come immediately after the sores and wounds on his previous followers (W-8). And finally, the Protestant apostasy of Luther (W-4) directly follows King Henry VIII's falling away from the Catholic Church (W-3).

Please note that even with the very accurate chronology of the ROC chart, some events can be slightly juxtaposed. Luther actually preceded Henry VIII by a few years, but follows him on the ROC chart. Similarly, we will see that Nazi Germany is placed ahead of Russian Communism on the ROC chart. In both instances, the events historically overlap each other. Looking ahead to future events, it's entirely possible that WWIII will begin **before** the great warning, although on the ROC chart, God's warning to mankind occurs first. Thus the prophet is making sure that no one becomes complacent and says, "I don't need to worry about nuclear attack; I haven't received God's promised warning yet."

Conversely, some paired events in the original sequence, which seem on the surface to be related, are shown to be completely different when examined in light of the ROC chart. The "rivers made blood" (B-7) are a plague upon the kingdom of the Antichrist, whereas the preceding "blood in the sea" (R-8) refers to decaying dead bodies, the casualties of war. The "hail, fire and blood" (W-3), the "mountain of fire" (R-3), and "Wormwood" (B-3) all fall from the sky and follow each other in the original text, but are, in fact, all decidedly unrelated events.

More verification comes when the apocalyptic story is retold according to the ROC chart and we find a dramatic buildup and gradual development not found in the original (see Appendix A). C. C. Martindale wrote about the original plan, "Why St. John arranged his material in this pattern I can form no conjecture."[3] For example, in Chapter 14, the punishment for taking the mark of the Beast and worshipping his image is to be cast into hell fire. Later on in Chapter 16, the punishment is much less severe, "a sore and grievous wound." This

---

[3] Martindale, C. C., S.J. *Saint John and the Apocalypse*, p. 75
    Rev. Martindale also wryly observes on page 109: "To seven angels are given seven bowls full of the 'last plagues' — last, that is, in this book which has already, at least three times, related the consummation of the world.

sequence is correctly reversed on the ROC chart. As we progress through the story of Revelation, both the punishments and the prizes should become greater, not less. (More on that later.)

And last but not least, St. John leaves a fascinating clue that the text is purposely meant to be unraveled and "sewn" back up again. In Chapter 16, the author inserts Verse 15, which is actually an unrelated side comment, between Verses 14 and 16 which describe Armagedon. Many other translators place parentheses around this verse and others simply move verse 15 after verse 16. But this was not accidental! Verse 15 is the "Rosetta Stone" of the Apocalypse. This is St. John's way of saying, "You must restructure the text to find the hidden secrets contained therein."

So why are the visions in the Book of Revelation as compiled by St. John out of order? Did the author purposely mix them up or did the Holy Spirit reveal them to St. John in a sequence that was meant to be unraveled only in these latter days? We will probably never know the answer except that it is becoming more and more critical that this prophetic work must be restructured into its correct chronological sequence in order to attain the true insights so necessary now in these Apocalyptic end-times.

In discussing these chapters of Revelation, I will not add or subtract one word to St. John's prophecies. St. John himself warns: "If any man shall add to these things, God shall add unto him the plagues written in this Book." St. John fully understands the temptation to clarify his writing because it's difficult to comprehend but he knows the answer lies in reorganizing, not editing. Therefore, I will simply rearrange the 36 segments of these fifteen end-times chapters in a horizontal sequence according to the ROC chart, rather than print them in a vertical sequence as traditionally found in your Bibles.

THE GREAT APOSTASY

W-1 — WHITE HORSE

6:1   And I saw that the Lamb had opened one of the seven seals, and I heard one of the four living creatures, as it were the voice of thunder, saying: Come, and see.

6:2   And I saw: and behold a white horse, and he that sat on him had a bow, and there was a crown given him, and he went forth conquering that he might conquer.

The First Horseman (the White Horse) which the Lamb (Christ) releases is the spirit of Apostasy. The bow indicates a struggle, although not as physically bloody as a sword. Heresy causes persecutions and martyrdom but not full scale war between nations. The color white points to a spiritual battle. The rider's crown proclaims victory and later on in Chapter 13, he indeed wins his war against the Saints, albeit only temporarily. This is the Great Apostasy which St. Paul declares must precede the advent of the Antichrist and the return of the Lord (2 Thes. 2:3). This figure cannot represent Christ, as some suggest, because Christ conquers with the two edged sword of His mouth, in other words, with His gospel, the Word of God.

Why does Christ release the Spirit of Apostasy? To test the saints and to separate the sheep from the goats. All four horsemen represent trials or tests for this last generation. Even though the four horsemen relentlessly attack all humanity, Christ releases them for our benefit. Unlike any previous generation, those who pass these extraordinary tests will reap an extraordinary reward: we will reign with Jesus on earth for a thousand peaceful years (the Millennium).

According to Roman Catholic canon law, there are two major kinds of Apostasy: falling away from the faith and renouncing Holy Orders or religious vows. It will be far more educational if the text immediately begins to explain the consequences of these apostasies. In St. John's original sequence, the White Horseman (Apostasy) is followed immediately by the three other horsemen: War, Famine and Death. Because eight pertinent events dealing with the two types of apostasy occur time-wise before the other horsemen, rearranging them according to the ROC chart places them in a more logical position following the White Horse. The next section, 6:9-11, reveals, far better than 6:3-4, those who are victims of the Great Apostasy.

W-2 — INNOCENT BLOOD

6:9   And when he had opened the fifth seal, I saw under the altar the souls of them that were slain for the word of God, and for the testimony which they held.

6:10   And they cried with a loud voice, saying: How long, O Lord (holy and true) do you not judge and avenge our blood on them that dwell on earth?

6:11   And white robes were given to every one of them; and it was said to them, that they should rest for a little time, till their fellow servants, and their brethren, who are to be slain, even as they, should be filled up.

Already here in the second segment we can discover the importance of rearranging the text. Chapter 6:3-8 refer to the 2nd, 3rd, and 4th horsemen (war, tribulation, and chastisement). However, St. John returns to an elaboration of the first horseman, Apostasy, with the opening of the fifth seal in verses nine through eleven (W-2). Since the Great Apostasy must occur before World War III, Tribulation, and Chastisement (R-1, B-1, and P-1), moving verses 9-11 to follow verses 1-2 gives a much more accurate chronology.

In the previous section (W-1), the White Horseman (Apostasy) carries a bow and goes forth to conquer. Here in W-2 of the ROC chart, we know right away who it is he conquers: "The souls of them that were slain for the word of God." In fact, the number one theme of the entire Apocalypse is martyrdom. This section definitely belongs at the beginning.

St. John also enumerates here another amazing fact: the exact time for the end of human history will be determined, not by wars, or natural calamities, or human devices but when God decides that enough martyrs have shed their blood! In these few short sentences of W-2, the author outlines the entire fantastic scope of his book.

The martyrs St. John describes here don't fit the mold of well-known martyrs in Church history because they "cry with a loud voice" for God to **avenge** their blood. The most famous last sentiment of dying martyrs has always been to ask God to **forgive** their tormentors. The first Christian martyr, St. Stephen exclaimed, "Lord, do not hold this crime against them." (Acts 7:59) Jesus, Our Lord, set the holy example as He prayed on the cross, "Father, forgive them for they know not what they do." (Luke 23:34)

God answers these martyrs of the Great Apostasy who are in heaven crying out for revenge, "Rest a little time until your fellow servants and brethren are slain." The question arises, are these "fellow servants" and "brethren" two different types of martyrs? "Brethren" indicates a close relationship. "Fellow servants", however, could include more than one category just as a butler is not a maid or a chauffeur. Evidently there are indeed several martyr types and later on we will see a third type who will return with Christ to set up His kingdom on earth (Millennium). The martyrs of the Great Apostasy which St. John sees are not like the early Christian saints who willingly gave their lives for Christ. Rather, these are the countless millions who have been murdered before their time, mostly in these latter days, by evil, satanic societies such as the Nazi holocaust, Stalin's Gulag, Pol Pot's killing fields, Mao's "cultural revolution" and, in our own day, legalized abortion. None of these victims chose to have their lives ended prematurely.

There are a few exceptions to the above, such as St. Maximillian Kolbe who voluntarily took the place of a condemned inmate at Auschwitz. But of all the twentieth and twenty-first century's unwilling martyrs, the loudest cries for vengeance without doubt come from aborted babies who never even get to see the light of day. God's plans for their innocent lives are completely thwarted. At least the voluntary martyrs live into adulthood and are free to make a decision to die for the Lord.

During the reign of the Antichrist, there will be many more martyrs willing to die for the Faith. Virtually every page of the Apocalypse chronicles this theme. Over and over, the Saints must choose martyrdom and death if they are to remain loyal to Christ. Over and over, the followers of the Antichrist increasingly devote their lives to evil and become evil's slaves. Despite at least nine plagues from God, no malfeasant follower of the Antichrist ever repents.

This generation, you and I included, are being given the same choices. To repeat a famous prophecy, "Many Saints have wanted to live in these times." Aren't we fortunate to be the actual ones to live these days and see the pages of the Apocalypse turn before our very eyes!

W-3 — HAIL, FIRE AND BLOOD

8:6   And the seven angels, who had the seven trumpets, prepared themselves to sound the trumpet.

8:7   And the first angel sounded the trumpet, and there followed hail and fire, mingled with blood, and it was cast on the earth, and the third part of the earth was burnt up, and the third part of the trees was burnt up, and all green grass was burnt up.

These verses from Chapter 8:6-7 deal with the Apostasy and should be moved following the Fifth Seal. They do not chronologically follow the Seventh Seal as in the original text. What is this strange trinity of "hail, blood and fire"? From our study of trinities, we recognize this as a structural trinity of solid, liquid and gas. Because this particular heresy exhibits all three parts of a trinity, that means it is complete and affects the entire society. By placing this event in its correct Apostasy sequence according to the ROC chart, we know the symbols must describe a spiritual, rather than an actual physical chastisement. Just as war is a physical chastisement, apostasy is a spiritual chastisement. Although there are some physical consequences, don't look up at the sky and expect to ever see real balls of fire, blood and hail mixed together!

Instead, this particular apostasy points to King Henry the Eighth who made himself "Pope" of England. When the hail destroys one-third of the earth and one-third of the trees, the reference is to King Henry destroying one-third of the Catholic churches, monasteries, and other beautiful buildings as well as the social welfare organizations which they housed. The blood refers to martyrs, such as St. Thomas More and St. Margaret Clitherow and the priests and nuns killed by King Henry. The fire represents the worst plague because nearly the entire English nation (all the green grass) lost their Catholic faith.

Henry the Eighth's most dubious distinction is that he murdered two of his six wives. Since the Pope wouldn't grant him a divorce, he invented "divorce, English style." Not that the popes of this era were paragons of virtue either. Be forewarned: when we stand before the judgment seat of God, no religion or denomination will stand with us. We answer for our own, not others, crimes or merits. An end times Antipope who proclaims that taking the mark of the Beast is no big deal will only succeed in dragging others down with him to hell. Hopefully, by this time, the last great Pope of the Catholic Church, Pope Peter II, will forcefully counter every satanic fallacy of the False Prophet and the "man of sin", the Antichrist.

W-4 — STINGING LOCUSTS

8:13   And I beheld, and heard the voice of one eagle flying through the midst of heaven, crying with a loud voice: Woe, woe, woe to the inhabitants of the earth: by reason of the rest of the voices of the three angels who are yet to sound the trumpet.

9:1   And the fifth angel sounded the trumpet, and I saw a star fall from heaven upon the earth, and there was given to him the key of the bottomless pit.

9:2   And he opened the bottomless pit and the smoke of the pit arose, as the smoke of a great furnace, and the sun and the air were darkened with the smoke of the pit.

9:3   And from the smoke of the pit there came out locusts upon the earth. And power was given to them as the scorpions of the earth have power;

The above verses from Chapter 9 continue the furor, confusion and unhappiness of apostasy, in this case another view of the Protestant reformation. The "star" that falls is Martin Luther and the "locusts" are his heretical followers. According to Canon Law, Luther's fall from faith was abandonment of his monastic vows.

From our rearrangement, we know that the locusts cannot be, for example, helicopters, as some have suggested, and when the sun is "darkened", it is not the real sun but the light of the Catholic faith. These heresies ultimately lead to our current suicidal culture of death: "They shall desire to die." Just as Henry the Eighth is a prefigure of the Antichrist, that is, a temporal leader who assumes religious authority, Martin Luther is a prefigure of the False Prophet, meaning a religious leader who apostatizes from the Catholic faith. The reign of the Antichrist and his False Prophet is a culmination of the Great Apostasy, the great falling away from Catholicism. It's not surprising that these two "reformers" are described side-by-side (W-3 and W-4) in the ROC chart. For an excellent description of this section (W-4), detail by detail, read Rev. Kramer's *The Book of Destiny* [4].

9:4   And it was commanded of them that they should not hurt the grass of the earth, nor any green thing or any tree, but only the men who have not the sign of God on their foreheads.

---

[4] Kramer, Rev. Herman Bernard, *The Book of Destiny*, p. 214-226.

9:5   And it was given unto them that they should not kill them, but that they should torment them five months; and their torment was as the torment of a scorpion when it strikes a man,

9:6   And in those days men shall seek death, and shall not find it; and they shall desire to die, and death shall fly from them.

9:7   And the shapes of the locusts were like unto horses prepared unto battle: and on their heads were, as it were, crowns like gold: and their faces were as the faces of men.

9:8   And they had hair as the hair of women; and their teeth were as lions:

9:9   And they had breastplates as breastplates of iron, and the noise of their wings was as the noise of chariots and many horses running to battle.

9:10   And they had tails like to scorpions, and there were stings in their tails; and their power was to hurt men five months, And they had over them

9:11   A king, the angel of the bottomless pit; whose name in Hebrew is Abaddon, and in Greek Apollyon; in Latin Exterminans.

9:12   One woe is past, and behold there come yet two woes more hereafter.

As in the previous section (W-3) the "green grass" and "trees" represent lay people and clergy whose faith is "hurt" by the spread of Lutherism. Not all the "green grass" is destroyed by Luther because, unlike England, about one half of the German people retained their Catholic faith. However those without a cross on their foreheads no longer will be able to profess the Apostle's Creed: "I believe in One, Holy, Catholic and Apostolic Church." Jesus was concerned about future fractured Christianity when He prayed for this last generation "that they all may be one." (Jn. 17:21)

The good news is that the Protestant heresy is short-lived — five months. The bad news is that each month lasts one century, but since Luther posted his 95 theses in 1517, those five centuries are almost finished. The Great Apostasy leads in the near future to World War III, followed by the Great Tribulation and the New World Disorder which is finally crushed through Divine Chastisement.

St. John's use of number repetition for emphasis will be apparent throughout Revelation. "Five months" is stated twice so as to alert the reader to its significance as a symbol for a longer time frame (five centuries). The "angel of the bottomless pit" (Satan) is given three names, Abaddon, Apollyon, and Exterminans to emphasize the threefold spiritual power of the devil in imitating the Divine Trinity. The "locusts" exhibit ten traits which could represent perversions of the Ten Commandments: the "hair like women" suggests adultery, the imitation ("as it were") crowns of gold indicate the usurpation of legitimate authority. The ten evil traits may also prefigure the ten evil world leaders who back the Antichrist.

Of the three "woes" in Revelation, this is the shortest in terms of number of words but the longest (500 years) in terms of calendar time. The ROC chart provides far more accurate chronology than the original organization, however, the new corrected time frame still should be regarded as only approximate.

W-5 — GREAT SIGN AND RED DRAGON

*12:1   And there appeared a great sign in heaven:
a woman clothed with the sun, and the moon under
her feet, and on her head a crown of twelve stars:*

*12:2   And she being with child, cried travailing
in birth, and was in pain to be delivered.*

*12:3   And there appeared another sign in heaven:
and behold, a great red dragon, having seven heads
and ten horns, and on his heads seven diadems,*

*12:4   And his tail drew the third part of the stars
of heaven, and cast them to the earth; and the dragon
stood before the woman, who was ready to be
delivered, that when she should be delivered,
he might devour her son.*

*12:5   And she brought forth a man child, who
was to rule all nations with an iron rod: and
her son was taken up to God, and to his throne:*

*12:6   And the woman fled into the wilderness,
where she had a place prepared by God, that
there they should feed her a thousand two hundred
and sixty days.*

The Great Apostasy continues with one-third of the Catholic priests (stars) falling with Martin Luther away from the Faith. Now we find out who it is that leads these heretics astray. No surprise here — it is Satan, the red dragon.

As the Protestant heresies have expanded over the past several hundred years, countless new denominations have appeared. Their chief contentions with the Catholic faith are: the authority of the Pope; the real presence of Jesus in the Holy Eucharist; and Mary's role in mankind's redemption. These are basically heresies against the divine powers of the Holy Trinity — Father, Son, and Holy Spirit respectively. Yet in 12:1-6, Mary's safety and reputation is protected by almighty God Himself in a "wilderness" for 1260 days (simultaneous with the length of time the Antichrist reigns).

Jesus said that in the end-times, there would be "signs in the sun, moon and the stars." (Luke 21:25) As we have learned, these stellar objects symbolize the Holy Trinity. Mary appears in St. John's vision surrounded by all three from head to toe.

The "great sign" of Mary in heaven "clothed with the sun" probably refers to her appearance at Fatima in 1917, or it may refer to a future "warning" or "miracle" so often prophesied about in private revelations of the past 50-60 years. In either case, Mary's predestined role in "crushing" the head of the "serpent" is prefigured here.

In the Fatima message of July 13, 1917, the Blessed Mother predicted that "The war (World War I) is going to end. (It did end the next year.) Another worse war will begin in the reign of Pius XI. (World War II began in 1938 as warned.) I shall come to ask for the consecration of Russia. (She fulfilled this promise to Sister Lucy, the seer of Fatima in her private appearance in Tuy, Spain in 1929.) Russia will spread her errors throughout the world, provoking wars and persecutions of the Church. The good will be martyred. Various nations will be annihilated." [5] At this time (2007) only the last of these prophecies has yet to occur.

The seven heads of her adversary, the dragon (Satan), undoubtedly represent spiritual temptations such as the seven deadly sins, while the ten heads stand for heresies, or sins against the Ten Commandments. The dragon with seven heads and ten horns is a diabolical precursor of the two later-appearing Beasts, each with seven heads and ten horns. The only apparent difference is that the diadems signifying authority are on the seven heads of the dragon and on the ten horns of the Beasts.

The "Woman" of the Apocalypse also represents the Church, especially those who honor Mary in these latter days. Mary has provided her children two powerful weapons with which to battle Satan and the Antichrist: the Rosary, an offensive weapon, and the Scapular, a defensive weapon. Since the Pope and bishops seem reluctant to consecrate Russia to the Immaculate Heart of Mary as requested by Mary of Sister Lucia and which would result in Russia's conversion, the

---

[5] Rev. John Ireland Gallery, *Mary vs Lucifer*, p. 118.

Rosary and Scapular will be our only spiritual swords of protection.

The desert place prepared by God in the wilderness for Mary and her (spiritual) seed is likely one of the places of protection. This safe haven will extend for a time period throughout the reign of the Antichrist, symbolically 1260 days. These "safe" zones may be caves, mountains, woods, or even your own home, if the Lord chooses to blind Satan as to your whereabouts.

But not everyone will be raptured or protected. It's clear that some and probably most will experience the days of tribulation and do battle with Satan and his minion, the Antichrist. When Jesus says, "The days will be shortened for the sake of the elect," (Matt. 24:22) obviously He must be referring to those "elect" believers who are "left behind." If all the "elect" were raptured or protected, as some maintain, there would be no need for Christ to "shorten the days."

W-6 — GOSPEL PREACHED

14:6   And I saw another angel flying through the midst of heaven, having the eternal gospel, to preach unto them that sit upon the earth, and over every nation, and tribe, and tongue, and people.

14:7   Saying with a loud voice: Fear the Lord, and give him honor, because the hour of his judgment is come; and adore you him, that made heaven and earth, the sea, and the fountains of water.

Just as the spirit of Apostasy introduced three related trials — Martyrdom and the heresies of Luther and King Henry the Eighth — a new "herald" angel (W-6) announces three more even worse events (W-7, W-8, and W-9) which are a result of the Great Apostasy. This angel cries out the summation of all true prophecy, "Repent, for the Kingdom of God is at hand."

Jesus prophesied that one of the signs of the end times would be the preaching of His words to all peoples: "And the gospel of the kingdom shall be preached in the whole world for a witness to all nations; and then will come the end." (Matt. 24-14) This prophecy began to be fulfilled in the first half of the twentieth century.

At the same time that Mary appeared to the children at Fatima as "the Woman clothed with the sun", a startling technical revolution in the electronic and communication media was taking place. The "angel" flying through the "midst of heaven" symbolizes this new means of spreading the gospel to the ends of the earth by radio and later, motion pictures and television. If you want to determine if the Christian radio station you listen to is Biblical, merely check it against the template in 14:7.

The airplane as a means of transportation also advanced at this time and missionaries were able to reach the remotest corners of the globe. Pope John Paul II visited more countries than all his predecessors put together. Only the invention of the printing press was as important for evangelization as the scientific advances of the last century.

The voice in the "midst of heaven" very possibly has a double meaning. An additional cogent interpretation is that the "angel" refers to the explosion of private revelations in the last 100-150 years. It does not seem likely that St. John would include the timeless but not extraordinary message, "Fear and honor God who made the heavens and earth," unless there was something most unusual and pertinent about the "angel" which delivers this message.

That the angel represents both electronic media and also private revelation can be supported by evidence in the Old Testament. Daniel says, for example, that knowledge would increase in the latter days (Dan. 12:4). Also, the latter days would be marked by "your young men having visions and your old men dreaming dreams." (Joel 2:28) One of the most important advantages of using symbolism is that the symbol, in this instance the "angel", can have multiple meanings at the same time.

W-7 — GRIEVOUS WOUND

15:1   And I saw another sign in heaven, great and wonderful: seven angels having the seven last plagues. For in them is filled up the wrath of God.

15:2   And I saw as it were a sea of glass mingled with fire, and them that had overcome the beast, and his image, and the number of his name, standing on the sea of glass, having the harps of God:

15:3   And singing the canticle of Moses, the servant of God, and the canticle of the Lamb saying: Great and wonderful are your works, O Lord God Almighty; just and true are your ways, O King of ages.

15:4   Who shall not fear you, O Lord, and magnify your name? For you only art holy: for all nations shall come, and shall adore in your sight, because your judgments are manifest.

15:5   And after these things I looked; and behold, the temple of the tabernacle of the testimony in heaven was opened:

15:6   And the seven angels came out of the temple having the seven plagues, clothed with clean and white linen, and girt about the breasts with golden girdles.

15:7   And one of the four living creatures gave to the seven angels seven golden bowls, full of the wrath of God, who lives for ever and ever.

15:8   And the temple was filled with smoke from the majesty of God, and from his power, and no man was able to enter into the temple, till the seven plagues of the seven angels were fulfilled.

16:1   And I heard a great voice out of the temple, saying to the seven angels: Go, and pour out the seven bowls of wrath of God upon the earth.

16:2   And the first went, and poured out his bowl upon the earth, and there fell a sore and grievous wound upon men, who had the character of the beast; and upon them that adored the image thereof.

St John uses the word "beast" here for the first time in our new ROC arrangement. "Beast" can refer to the later appearing "beast from the sea" (Antichrist), the "beast from the earth" (False Prophet), or the "beast from the abyss" (New World Tyranny).

Here in W-7 the "beast" stands for Adolf Hitler. Hitler introduced the chief horrifying attribute of Socialism, the mass murder of your own citizenry, a phenomenon that was perfected in the twentieth century and has reached its peak today in the form of abortion, the mass murder of infants in the womb. It is significant to note the terrible effects of apostasy because the demon-possessed Hitler was at one time a Catholic altar boy. The two groups of martyrs in this segment refer to the millions of Jews and Christians murdered in Nazi concentration camps. The former "sing the canticle of Moses" while the latter "sing the canticle of the Lamb (Christ)."

Hitler also anticipated the Antichrist by promoting images of himself which all loyal citizens were expected to adulate. I remember seeing countless movies of World War II in which mesmerized Germans salute huge portraits of "der Fuehrer" with shouts of "Heil Hitler." We can deduce from the text that these Nazi images of the "Beast" were not as soul destroying as will be the eventual image of the Antichrist because the penalty was not as severe. The "sore and grievous wound" symbolizes the military defeat of Germany. Later on the penalty for worshipping the image of the final "Beast" (Antichrist) will be much greater — it will mean eternal damnation for individuals, and annihilation for nations.

By contrast, the punishment for subjects of the earlier precursor of the Antichrist, Henry VIII, was less than for those of Hitler: hail, blood and fire. God's chastisement for the abortion crimes of Capitalism (Babylon) will be worse. As the murder rate increases, so will the eventual sufferings of the perpetrators.

God's punishments become more intense as mankind progresses into ever greater apostasy. St. John is warning us that the final Chastisement will be exponentially worse, just as Hitler's was much more severe than Henry VIII's.

On the positive side, the martyrs who overcame this forerunner beast, Hitler, are depicted in heaven. Later on, those who overcome the ultimate beast, Antichrist, will gain the millennial privilege, returning with Christ for the thousand year reign of peace.

Why has no one else ever interpreted these verses as references to Hitler and Nazi Germany? First, because there was no ROC chart to indicate the time line for St. John's visions. Second, the author kept the descriptions obscure on purpose. Why? Because that tragedy did not have to happen! The Blessed Mother warned in 1917 at Fatima, "If people do not stop offending God, another and worse war will begin." If the world had listened to Mary, WWII could have been avoided and St. John's prophecies would have had meaning for only the very end times of the Antichrist.

W-8 — GOD BLASPHEMED

16:10   And the fifth angel poured out his bowl upon the seat of the beast; and his kingdom became dark, and they gnawed their tongues for pain:

16:11   And they blasphemed the God of heaven, because of their pains and wounds, and did not penance for their works.

In this brief section another evil empire of the twentieth century is indicated: Communist Russia. In the previous segment, while Hitler's Socialism was being defeated, an even worse form was developing in Russia under an even worse dictator, Joseph Stalin. Mary's warning about Russia has come true and the first "seat of the beast", the current capital of world Socialism/Communism, is Moscow. Again, it is interesting to note the apostasy in ruthless Stalin's own personal life: he was for a time a seminarian in the Orthodox faith. Yet ultimately he practiced the number one hallmark of Socialism, mass murder, to a greater degree than Adolf Hitler.

The "kingdom which became dark" refers to the loss of the great Russian culture of the nineteenth century. Few countries can match the tremendous outburst of genius in men like Tolstoy, Dostoyevsky, Tchaikovsky and many others. Gifted artists of the twentieth century like Rachmaninoff and Solzhenitsyn left or were exiled from Communist Russia while the works of others like Pasternak were often suppressed. The "darkness" extended to religion and the enforced atheism of this evil empire is expressed by St. John as "they blasphemed the God of heaven."

Besides practicing atheistic blasphemy, the Communists in Russia have never done "penance" for their "works" which refers mainly to their reign of terror and Stalin's Gulag. That this section describes Russia is again not indisputable because these trials could have been prevented. Mary said at Fatima, "If people listen to my requests, Russia will be converted and there will be peace." If Mary's requests for the conversion of Russia continue to go unheeded, St. John's prophecies in the next segment will come to pass and the world wide Communist revolution will advance from Russia to Italy.

This section about Russia (W-8) and the previous one about Germany (W-7) form a related pair which follow each other, similar to the paired sections about Henry VIII and Martin Luther (W-3 and W-4). In the previous section (W-7), the First Angel with a bowl dumps his plague on the followers of Hitler while here in W-8 the Fifth Angel dumps his bowl of plagues on the seat of the Beast (Moscow). We will be finding several more obviously paired sections which serve as further indications that our understanding of the Apocalypse is greatly enhanced by restructuring the text according to the ROC chart.

W-9 — HARLOT ASTRIDE BEAST

17:1   And there came one of the seven angels, who had the seven bowls, and spoke with me, saying: Come, I will show you the condemnation of the great harlot who sits upon many waters.

17:2   With whom the kings of the earth have committed fornication; and they who inhabit the earth, have been made drunk with the wine of her prostitution.

17:3   And he took me away in the spirit into the desert. And I saw a woman sitting upon a scarlet colored beast, full of names of blasphemy, having seven heads and ten horns.

17:4   And the woman was clothed round in purple and scarlet, and gilded with gold, and precious stones, and pearls, having a golden cup in her hand, full of the abomination and filthiness of her fornication.

17:5   And on her forehead a name was written: A mystery: Babylon the great, the mother of the fornications and abominations of the earth.

17:6   And I saw the woman drunk with the blood of the saints, and with the blood of the martyrs of Jesus. And when I had seen her, I wondered with great admiration.

17:7   And the angel said to me: Why do you wonder? I will tell you the mystery of the woman, and of the beast which carries her, which has the seven heads and ten horns.

We have now arrived at one of the great turning points of history, the end of the Great Apostasy. Satan has seduced all he can through the temptations of heresy and the world is divided into two hostile camps, neither one of which merits any approval. In order to capture more souls, Satan must precipitate the trials and horrors of World War III which will bring about the full reign of the "Beast from the abyss" — the New World Tyranny.

One of the hostile camps is depicted as a harlot who personifies decadent Capitalism. She rides on and controls the other hostile camp, the Red Beast of atheistic Communism. The Socialist/Communist countries resent the harlot's commanding position and the stage is set for violent conflict.

One of the overriding themes of the Book of Revelation is conflict. Thirty-three of the thirty-six sections describe some sort of struggle. Nine describe evil versus evil, the "Harlot" against the "Beast from the abyss" (W-9, R-1, R-2, R-3, R-4, R-6, R-9), while twenty-three depict good versus evil. In this latter category are:

- Angels vs followers of two Beasts: (W-7, W-8, R-2, R-3, R-4, R-7, R-8, B-6, B-7)
- Heretics vs Saints: (W-1, W-2, W-3, W-4)
- Two Beasts vs Saints and Two Witnesses: (B-1, B-2, B-4, B-5)
- Beast (Antichrist) vs Lamb: (B-8, B-9, P-1, P-6, P-9)
- Dragon vs Woman (Mary) and her seed: (W-5)
- Michael vs Dragon: (R-5)

Of these struggles between good and evil, sixteen result in victories for the good side, while seven are losses. The only three events which do not show conflict are W-6, the Angel preaching the Gospel, B-3, the Fall of Wormwood, and P-5, 144,000 Saved Virgins.

A common fallacy of previous interpreters of the Book of Revelation is that one of the antagonists, the harlot, represents the Roman Catholic Church. Ever since I can remember, and I'm nearing seventy, I've heard the phony claim of many a Protestant televangelist that "the Catholic Church is the whore of Babylon." The primary basis for this fiction is that St. John says the Harlot sits on "seven mountains", but just a few paragraphs earlier, he states that she sits on "many waters." This is her true geographical location. Therefore, the real whore of Babylon refers to Capitalism, the adopted economic system for many of the world's "peoples, and nations, and tongues" (many waters). (17:15)

Admittedly, one of the meanings for the seven mountains is that they stand for the seven hilled city of Rome, but that indicates the location of the "seat of the beast." The current (2007) "seat of the beast" is Moscow. Rome will become the future capital of the Antichrist's One World Tyranny and One World religion, not Capitalism's capital. The Harlot "sitting" on the mountains means that she maintains authority over them — that is, Capitalism exercises political and economic control over worldwide Socialist/Communism.

The true location of the Harlot on "many waters" not only symbolizes her geographical placement but also her laissez-faire economic and libertarian political characteristics. "Many waters" means there is no one central authority. Unfortunately, this freedom of Western culture, having lost its moral compass, has degenerated into licentiousness, child sacrifice (abortion) and idolatry (God is money).

Conversely, the one symbolic location for the capitol of Socialist/Communism, "the seat of the Beast", not only indicates that Rome will eventually earn that designation, but also that this totalitarian system espouses centralized political and economic authority. This type of system often seems to degenerate into the "cult of personality", emperor worship, and blasphemy. The Antichrist will inevitably plaster his image throughout the world even more than Castro, Mao, Stalin or Lenin.

The image which the Antichrist promotes may actually turn out to be one of these former "heroes" of the revolution. Already, we honor Lenin's birthday by celebrating "Earth Day". It's not too far-fetched for Disney to concoct a digital masterpiece of Nicolai Lenin spouting "great things" from televised images around the globe. But woe to you if you "Heil Hitler" this, or any other possible image of the "Beast" as it speaks.

THE BEAST FROM THE ABYSS

17:8   The beast which you saw, was, and is not, and shall come up out of the bottomless pit, and go into destruction: and the inhabitants of the earth (whose names are not written in the book of life from the foundation of the world) shall wonder, seeing the beast, that was, and is not.

17:9   And here is the understanding, that has wisdom. The seven heads are seven mountains, upon which the woman sits, and they are seven kings.

17:10   Five are fallen, one is, and the other is not yet come: and when he shall come, he must remain a short time.

17:11   And the beast that was, and is not: the same is also the eighth: and is of the seven and goes into destruction.

17:12   And the ten horns, which you saw, are ten kings: who have not yet received a kingdom, but shall receive power as kings one hour after the beast.

17:13   These have one design, and their strength and power they shall deliver to the beast.

17:14   These shall fight with the Lamb, and the Lamb shall overcome them; because he is Lord of lords, and King of kings, and they that are with him are called, and elect, and faithful.

17:15   And he said to me: The waters which you saw where the harlot sits, are peoples, and nations, and tongues.

17:16   And the ten horns, which you saw on the beast, these shall hate the harlot, and shall make her desolate and naked, and shall eat her flesh, and shall burn her with fire.

17:17   For God has given into their hearts to do that which pleases him: that they give their kingdom to the beast till the words of God be fulfilled.

17:18   And the woman which you saw, is the great city, a kingdom which has dominion over the kings of the earth.

The other great antagonist described in section W-9, and which develops as a consequence of the Great Apostasy, is the worldwide Communist Empire, the seventh "Beast". Socialist/Communism is the last of seven world tyrannies, and is the same as the last end-times Beast in the prophet Daniel's vision, the fourth Beast which grinds up and treads down all other nations (Dan. 7:19).

Currently (2007) this seventh head of the Beast has been "killed", which we smugly term "the fall of the Soviet Union." This "fall" is pure propaganda, but it very accurately fulfills St. John's prophecy that one of the heads of the Beast (number seven) would be destroyed and later be resurrected as the eighth head of the Beast. Everyone, except knowledgeable Christians, will be amazed at Communism's revival after World War III and will wonder seeing the "Beast that was, and is not, and goes to destruction." The prophecy that "one of its heads will be slain" refers symbolically to both the first "Beast from the abyss" (World Tyranny) as well as to the second "Beast from the sea" (Antichrist).

The ten horns on the Beast of St. John's vision, represent a ten-nation confederacy, probably the new godless European Union, which also resents Capitalist's control of the world's economy. They will support Communism's military conquest of Capitalism, but their real goal is the end of Christianity. The Antichrist's One World Tyranny and One World Religion will succeed in destroying all visible, at least outwardly visible, traces of the Church. Of course, when they decide to take on the Lamb (Jesus), that's when the Antichrist, his False Prophet, and the ten leaders of his political union, will all be violently thrust into the lake of fire (Hell).

The "ten horns" or ten nation confederacy are derived primarily from the ancient Roman empire, but since "ten" is a complete number in prophecy, it means that all the nations of the world will be unified into a One World Tyranny. When they give their kingdom to the "Beast", it means that Italy goes Communist and the capital of international Socialist/Communism will be removed from Moscow to Rome.

Rome will become the second "seat of the Beast" and will eventually be replaced by Jerusalem, the last Beast headquarters. If you look at a globe or a map, the cities of Moscow, Rome and Jerusalem form the points of a nearly perfect equilateral triangle.

We are beginning to understand that there really is a chronological sequence to the Book of Revelation after all. The Great Apostasy builds from the early martyrs, to the heresies of Luther and Henry VIII, to the Fatima warnings, to world wide electronic communication, to Hitler's Nazi dictatorship and finally to the spread of Communism. In the original text these events are scattered throughout, but when we read them in the correct ROC chart sequence, their succession seems almost inevitable.

The next nine segments, which are led off by the Red Horseman of War, describe in more detail the great war, World War III, between

Communism (the Beast from the abyss) and Capitalism (the Harlot). St. John writes more about this cataclysmic event than any other in the entire Book of Revelation. God allows this horrible chastisement on humanity because we refuse to renounce apostasy and the fruits thereof, particularly abortion, the innocent blood which cries out to God for revenge (Rev. 6:10).

THE GREAT WAR

R-1 — RED HORSE

*6:3   And when he had opened the second seal,
I heard the second living creature, saying:
Come and see.*

*6:4   And there went out another horse that was
red: and to him that sat thereon, it was given that he
should take peace from the earth, and that they should
kill one another, and a great sword was given to him.*

Although much innocent blood (both martyrs and abortion) was
spilled during the great apostasy, even greater mass killing of the general
populace now follows the most fearsome horse of the Apocalypse, the
Red Horse of War. World War III demonstrates that there is no Hegelian
synthesis between the thesis, Capitalism, and its antithesis, Communism.
The "Beast", Socialist/Communism will prevail.

R-2 — GOD'S WRATH

*6:12   And I saw, when he had opened the sixth
seal, and behold there was a great earthquake, and
the sun became black as sackcloth of hair: and the
whole moon became as blood.*

*6:13   And the stars from heaven fell upon the earth,
as the fig tree casts its green figs when it is shaken by
a great wind:*

*6:14   And the heaven departed as a scroll when it
is rolled together: and every mountain, and the
islands were moved out of their places.*

*6:15   And the kings of the earth, and the princes,
and tribunes, and the rich, and the strong, and every
bondsman, and every freeman, hid themselves in the
dens and in the rocks of mountains:*

> *6:16   And they say to the mountains and the rocks:*
> *Fall on us, and hide us from the face of him that sits*
> *upon the throne and from the wrath of the Lamb:*
>
> *6:17   For the great day of their wrath is come, and*
> *who shall be able to stand?*

This event is not World War III itself but a preliminary trial. Just before the Great War, Almighty God in His mercy sends mankind a fearful warning. The earthquake is a major disaster affecting the entire planet, since all the people, rich and poor alike, try to hide. This warning is well described by many "seers" of the Blessed Virgin.[6] It can also be found in Isaiah 34:4:

> "And all the host of heaven shall be
> dissolved and the heavens shall be rolled together as a
> scroll. And all their host shall fall down, as the leaf
> falls off from the vine and as a falling fig from the fig
> tree."

According to St. Jacinta's description of the warning, "There is a secret of heaven and another one of earth, and the latter is terrifying. It will seem as though it were the end of the world. In the cataclysm, everything will be separated from the sky, which will turn white as snow."

The falling stars (6:13) are not demons or apostate clergy in this case, but probably meteorites or particles from a passing asteroid or comet, hence the need for people to hide in rocks or caves. Some believe that the "green" figs means that the warning occurs in winter.[7]

Since this warning follows the Red Horse (War) rather than the White Horse (Apostasy), we know that the earthquake, the bloody moon, and the blackened sun are real and not symbols of a spiritual chastisement. These are the signs in the sun, moon and stars which Jesus said would presage His return (Mark 12:24,25). Notice that everyone is terrified, from king to slaves, but not the faithful Christians who were persecuted during the Great Apostasy. They will recognize God's anger and rejoice at the coming destruction of Babylon (Capitalism).

The purpose of this warning is to stave off World War III and the final Great Chastisement. Since the Great War follows immediately, God's mercy evidently goes unheeded. World War III has been predicted by Our Lady of Fatima and will result in the "annihilation of nations." Mary had also prophesied in 1917 that if the people did not repent, World War II would break out. Is there any evidence today that

---

[6] Joseph A. Pelletier, Our Lady Comes to Garabandal, p. 148.
[7] C. Marystone, The Shepherds Are Lost, p. 110.

repentance has increased enough to prevent Mary's 90-year and St. John's 2000-year prophecies of the most terrifying of wars, WWIII, from being cataclysmically fulfilled?

R-3 — MOUNTAIN OF FIRE

8:8   And the second angel sounded the trumpet: and as it were a great mountain, burning with fire, was cast into the sea, and the third part of the sea became blood:

8:9   And the third part of those creatures died, which had life in the sea, and the third part of the ships was destroyed.

Here we first observe the surprise nuclear attack which starts WWIII. The second angel's trumpet announces the dropping of an ICBM (Mountain of Fire, 8:8) and is part of the destruction of Babylon, as explained later in detail. Again, the symbolism is of a physical chastisement, not spiritual. This is not where "green grass" or the "sea" represents people. Here it is real sea creatures and real ships which are destroyed. Once more our ROC chart showing the text rearrangement aids in our understanding of St. John's symbolism.

According to the Bayside prophecies, another reference to an ICBM may be found in the Old Testament Book of Zechariah 5:1-4. The prophet sees a flying "volume" twenty cubits by ten cubits which is about the size of a nuclear-tipped ICBM. The angel tells Zechariah, "This is the curse that enters into the house of the thief, and to the house of him that swears falsely by my name; and it shall remain in the midst of his house and shall consume it, with the timber thereof, and the stones thereof."

As we have seen with the narration of Hitler, Stalin, Luther and Henry VIII, the chronology of even the very accurate ROC chart may not be exact. Therefore, don't become complacent thinking that WWIII cannot break out before the warning. The warning could very well occur **after** the sudden surprise attack and be God's way of admonishing mankind to stop the violence.

R-4 — HUGE ARMY

9:13   And the sixth angel sounded the trumpet: and I heard a voice from the four horns of the golden altar, which is before the eyes of God,

9:14   Saying to the sixth angel, who had the

trumpet: Loose the four angels, who are bound in the great river Euphrates.

9:15 And the four angels were loosed, who were prepared for an hour, and a day, and a month, and a year: for to kill the third part of men.

9:16 And the number of the army of the horsemen was twenty thousand times ten thousand. And I heard the number of them.

9:17 And thus I saw the horses in the vision: and they that sat on them, had breastplates of fire and of hyacinth and brimstone, and the heads of the horses were as the heads of lions: and from their mouths proceeded fire, and smoke, and brimstone.

9:18 And by these three plagues was slain the third part of men, by the fire and by the smoke and by the brimstone, which issued out of their mouths.

9:19 For the power of the horses is in their mouths, and in their tails. For their tails are like to serpents, and have heads: and with them they do hurt.

9:20 And the rest of the men, who were not slain by these plagues, did not do penance from the works of their hands, that they should not adore devils, and idols of gold, and silver, and brass, and stone, and wood, which neither can see, nor hear, nor walk:

9:21 Neither did they penance from their murders, nor from their fornications, nor from their thefts.

The trumpet of the sixth angel (R-4) announces the second major event of World War III: an invasion of the Middle East by China and Russia. The fire, smoke and brimstone (a trinity which connotes charcoal, sulfur and saltpeter, the ingredients of gunpowder) indicates conventional warfare which must be extensive since one-third of mankind are killed (or perhaps just one-third of those living in the area). Certainly all Western armies still deployed in Iraq (Tigris and Euphrates) and throughout the Middle East will be annihilated.

Just as the "locusts" involved in the spiritual warfare of the Great Apostasy could not be "helicopters", here the reverse is true. The "horses" which St. John describes in this vision most likely represent modern, mechanized weapons of war. The men they maim and kill die real physical, not spiritual, deaths.

As terrifying as World War III is, people do not repent. St. John lists the ten sins which require repentance. The symbolic number "10" indicates a complete and thorough lack of repentance. Jesus' end-times separation of the sheep from the goats will be decisive, tolerating no middle ground. Following the 9-11 terrorist attacks in New York City, the churches across America were filled. A few weeks thereafter, people showed what short memories they have and, soon, with their recovered sense of security, forgot their God, the source of all goodness, and our houses of worship returned to half empty. This lack of repentance will pave the way for the tribulation period and the final chastisement.

The "hour, day, month, and year" phraseology (9:15) for the start of the war shows that it is permitted by God and signifies His judgment on an apostate generation. The "one hour" also indicates how suddenly and unexpectedly World War III will break out, just when everyone is crying "peace and security".

Although the "one hour" indicates a sudden, shocking beginning, it does not symbolize the length of the war. An invasion by a 200-million man army will require many weeks and months to carry out, perhaps years. It's out of this confusion and chaos of continual warfare that the nations will turn to the Antichrist despite his One World Tyranny and depraved leadership.

R-5 — WOMAN FLEES DRAGON

12:7   And there was a great battle in heaven: Michael and his angels fought with the dragon, and the dragon fought, and his angels:

12:8   And they prevailed not, neither was their place found any more in heaven.

12:9   And that great dragon was cast out, the old serpent, who is called the devil, and Satan, who seduces the whole world, and he was cast forth unto the earth, and his angels were thrown down with him.

12:10   And I heard a loud voice in heaven, saying: Now is come salvation, and strength, and the kingdom of our God, and the power of his Christ: because the accuser of our brethren is cast forth, who accused them before our God day and night.

12:11   And they overcame him by the blood of the Lamb, and by the word of their testimony, and they loved not their lives unto death.

12:12   Therefore rejoice, O you heavens, and you that dwell therein; woe to the earth, and to the sea, because the devil is come down unto you, having great wrath, knowing that he has but a short time.

Here we are in the middle of World War III and an interesting interlude takes place. First, St. John tells the familiar story of Satan's defeat at the hands of the Archangel Michael and his expulsion from heaven. Next, the author reviews the Great Apostasy wherein the martyrs for the faith overcame Satan through the blood of the Lamb. By verse 12, we are already caught up to the very end because we are told the devil knows "he has but a short time."

> *12:13   And after the dragon saw that he was cast unto the earth, he persecuted the woman, who brought forth the man child:*
>
> *12:14   And there were given to the woman, two wings of a great eagle, that she might fly into the desert to her place, where she is nourished for a time, and times, and half a time, from the face of the serpent.*
>
> *12:15   And the serpent cast out of his mouth, after the woman, water, as it were a river; that he might cause her to be carried away by the river.*
>
> *12:16   And the earth helped the woman, and the earth opened her mouth, and swallowed up the river, which the dragon cast out of his mouth.*
>
> *12:17   And the dragon was angry against the woman: and went to make war with the rest of her seed, which keep the commandments of God, and have the testimony of Jesus Christ.*
>
> *12:18   And he stood upon the sand of the sea.*

Now the narrative diverges into several different possible meanings. First, the river with which the dragon seeks to drown Mary may represent the many blasphemies constantly pouring out from our satanic media and Hollywood. These blasphemies mock her Perpetual Virginity, her Immaculate Conception, her Holy Images, her Divine Maternity and her Catholic devotions. Verse 17 makes it clear that the last great conflict, begun with the first horseman (the White Horse) of the Apocalypse is essentially a war between Satan and the spiritual children of Mary.

Second, the "Woman" does not just represent Mary but also her spiritual children who are protected during the Great Tribulation period. Either or both interpretations of this passage are correct. The "earth" which helps Mary represents the "culture" of the gentiles. Sometimes this culture is a force for good, sometimes it produces evil results. It's the same "earth" (W-3) of which King Henry VIII destroys one third, and the same "earth" from which springs the False Prophet (B-5).

Even as decadent a culture as ours refuses to favorably acknowledge personal attacks on Mary, the Mother of our Lord. When the Brooklyn Art Museum exhibited a painting of Mary smeared with elephant dung and covered with images of women's private parts cut out of porn magazines, the public was incensed. Six-pack-Joe may not know what art is but he sure knows what hate speech is when he sees it.

St. John's vision may also be interpreted as a replay of the fall of mankind in the Garden of Eden. In this case, Mary reveals to humanity what Adam and Eve's reaction to Satan and the river of lies spewing from his mouth should have been, namely flight. Later on, the author tells his readers that we must "flee" the society of Babylon the Harlot (Capitalism) if we want to avoid her trials.

R-6 — BABYLON IS FALLEN

14:8   And another angel followed, saying: That great Babylon is fallen, is fallen; which made all nations to drink of the wine of the wrath of her fornication.

This 2nd Herald Angel (R-6) shifts the descriptions of war to the next four events which are more detailed images of the fall of Babylon. The phrase "is fallen, is fallen" indicates a double or twin event. Later on in Chapter 18:6, punishment is "rendered double" to Babylon according to her works. The terrorist attacks of 9-11 would fit this "double" description, an event foretold exactly 11 years prior to the date in the Bayside prophecies. More likely, however, the twin events refer to the two-pronged land and sea attack by the forces of the Beast from the abyss (Socialist/Communism) and the ten-nation confederation.

R-7 — BLOOD IN SEA

16:3   And the second angel poured out his bowl upon the sea, and there came blood as it were of a dead man; and every living soul died in the sea.

The sea war against Babylon (R-7) has already been alluded to when the ICBM attack destroys one third of the life in the sea, perhaps the Mediterranean Sea. The "dead man's blood" points to the resulting overwhelming decay and pestilence which now kills the rest of the sea creatures.

R-8 — EUPHRATES DRIED UP

16:12   And the sixth angel poured out his bowl upon that great river Euphrates; and dried up the water thereof, that a way might be prepared for the kings from the rising of the sun.

This second, land war phase (R-8) of the two pronged attack was also previously mentioned. Here St. John seems to be saying that the huge Chinese army will cross the Euphrates in a somewhat fantastic fashion on a dry river bed! Perhaps history will repeat itself. In the Book of Daniel, the prophet tells Belshazzar, the King of Babylon, that his kingdom is about to fall (Dan. 5:24-27). Daniel reads the "writing on the wall" where the angel of the Lord writes, "You have been weighed in the balance and found wanting." That night, Belshazzar's enemies, the Medes and Persians under Cyrus, gained entrance to the city by walking on the dry bed of the Euphrates "under" the walls of the city since they had successfully diverted the river upstream. The three sections, R-6, R-7, and R-8, are very short and basically repetitious of earlier World War III episodes. They are really unnecessary and could easily be tacked on to other passages, except for one reason: St. John needs them in order to fill out his nine segment pattern of events relating to each of the Four Horsemen. This pattern is crucial because it allows the book to be unraveled and reassembled in a logical and chronological sequence.

R-9 — FALL OF BABYLON

18:1   And after these things I saw another angel coming down from heaven, having great power: and the earth was enlightened with his glory.

18:2   And he cried out with a strong voice, saying: Babylon the great is fallen, is fallen: and is become the habitation of devils, and the hold of every unclean spirit, and the hold of every unclean and hateful bird:

18:3   Because all nations have drunk of the wine of the wrath of her fornication: and the kings of the earth have committed fornication with her: and the merchants of the earth have been made rich by the abundance of her delicacies.

18:4   And I heard another voice from heaven, saying: Go out from her, my people: that you be not partakers of her sins, and that you receive not of her plagues.

18:5   For her sins have reached even to heaven,
and the Lord has remembered her iniquities.

18:6   Render to her as she also has rendered to
you: and double unto her double according to her
works: in the cup, wherein she has mingled, mingle
unto her double.

18:7   As much as she has glorified herself,
and lived in delicacies, so much torment and sorrow
give you to her: because she says in her heart:
I sit a queen, and am not a widow: and sorrow I
shall not see.

18:8   Therefore shall her plagues come in one day,
death, and mourning, and famine, and she shall be
burnt with fire: because God is strong, who shall
judge her.

Chapter 18 (R-9) describes in greater detail the single most important event in the entire Apocalypse: the destruction of Babylon (World War III). First it should be noted that most commentators completely misinterpret the whore of Babylon and the Beast she rides on as somehow interconnected. This is false. Babylon represents perverted Capitalism riding on and exercising control over the Red Bear, or atheistic Communism, which resents this domination.

Neither of the two combatants of World War III are worthy of our sympathies. The Capitalist whore is "full of abomination and the filthiness of her fornication", a perfect description for the "sexual revolution". The Communist Beast is "full of the names of blasphemies." Yet God will allow the blasphemous, anti-Christian forces to defeat the "Christian in name only" Capitalist societies.

Many people will find it preposterous that God would punish the Capitalist nations, most of whom profess a nominal Christianity. But how many times in the Old Testament did God punish His most favorite nation on all the earth, Israel? The answer is, "To whom much has been given, much will be expected." The major sins of our morally corrupt West are luxurious riches, idols of materialism, and fornication (sexual sins).

Although it is God who judges Capitalist Babylon, the "death, mourning, famine and fire" do not come, at least at this point, as a heaven sent chastisement of fire and brimstone. The instrument God chooses to punish the decadent West is the nuclear might of Communist Russia with the support of the ten nation successors to the Roman Empire.

18:9   And the kings of the earth, who have committed fornication, and lived in delicacies with her, shall weep, and bewail themselves over her, when they shall see the smoke of her burning:

18:10   Standing afar off for fear of her torments, saying: Woe! woe! that great city, Babylon, that mighty city: for in one hour is your judgment come.

18:11   And the merchants of the earth shall weep and mourn over her: for no man shall buy their merchandise any more:

18:12   Merchandise of gold, and silver, and of precious stones, and pearls, and of fine linen, and purple, and of silk, and scarlet, and all thyine wood, and all manner of vessels of ivory, and all manner of vessels of precious stone, and of brass, and iron, and marble,

18:13   And cinnamon and of odors and ointment, and frankincense, and wine, and oil, and fine flour, and wheat, and beasts, and sheep and horses, and chariots, and slaves, and souls of men.

18:14   And the fruits of the desire of your soul are departed from you, and all fat and goodly things are perished from you, and they shall no more find them.

18:15   The merchants of these things, who were made rich, shall stand afar off from her, for fear of her torments, weeping and mourning

18:16   And saying: Woe! woe! that great city, which was clothed with fine linen, and purple, and scarlet, and was gilded with gold, and precious stones, and pearls:

18:17   For in one hour are so great riches come to naught: and every shipmaster, and every one that sails into the lake, and mariners, and they that work at sea, stood afar off,

18:18   And cried out, seeing the place of her burning, saying: What city is like to this great city?

18:19   And they cast dust upon their heads, and cried out, weeping and mourning, saying: Woe! woe! that great city, wherein all were made rich, who had ships at sea, by reason of her prices: for in one hour she is made desolate.

Verses 9-19 demonstrate clearly how ludicrous it is to consider Babylon as the Catholic Church. St. John takes a lot of time thoroughly describing the Capitalist nature of Babylon. There can be no mistaking the trinity of evils which offends God about Capitalism: "your merchants, your sorceries, your shedding of innocent blood." (18:23-24) He knows what He is doing. Sometimes you have to punish even your favorite children if you intend to bring them back to their senses.

Following World War III, the new lone superpower will be Russia (the scarlet Beast), supported by China and the ten nations of the European Union. It is possible by this time that the United States and other capitalist countries will avoid much of the destruction by freely electing a far left government which will either unilaterally disarm or give their full military support to the New World Disorder.

This Socialist/Communist One World Tyranny will be the greatest and last world empire. The first five (Persian, Greek, Egyptian, Chaldean and Assyrian) were "past", meaning before John's time, and the one that "is" represents the Roman Empire which was contemporaneous with the Saint. The one which is to come, Socialism/Communism, the seventh head, which will suffer a "fatal" wound, and then come back to life as the eighth Beast, is this final tyrannical, New World Empire .

As we previously noted, we are constantly propagandized about the "collapse" of the Soviet Union and that Communism is "dead". This concept actually fulfills the prophecy that one of the heads would be slain and then healed, "the Beast that was and is not and shall go to destruction." People will wonder at this resurrection and say, "Who is like the Beast and who shall be able to fight him." Russia will win World War III, but St. John says that Christians will not be surprised at Communism's resurgence, mainly because only we will understand that Russia is both the seventh and eighth Beast.

> *18:20   Rejoice over her, you heaven, and you holy apostles, and prophets: for God has judged your judgment on her.*
>
> *18:21   And a mighty angel took up a stone, as it were a great millstone, and cast it into the sea, saying: With this violence shall Babylon, that great city, be thrown down, and shall now be found no more.*
>
> *18:22   And the voice of harpers, and of musicians, and of them that play on the pipe, and on the trumpet, shall no more be heard in you: and no craftsman of any art whatsoever shall be found any more in you: and the sound of a mill shall be heard no more in you:*
>
> *18:23   And the light of a lamp shall shine no more in you; and the voice of the bridegroom and bride*

shall be heard no more in you: for your merchants were the great men of the earth, for all nations have been deceived by your sorceries.

18:24   And in her has been found the blood of prophets and of saints: and of all who were slain upon the earth.

19:1   After these things I heard as it were the voice of many multitudes in heaven, saying: Alleluia: salvation, and glory, and power is to our God:

19:2   For true and just are his judgments, who has judged the great harlot, which corrupted the earth with her fornication, and has revenged the blood of his servants, at her hands.

19:3   And again they said: Alleluia. And her smoke ascends for ever and ever.

19:4   And the four and twenty ancients, and the four living creatures, fell down and adored God, that sits upon the throne, saying: Amen: Alleluia.

This very long section (R-9) detailing the annihilation of Capitalism (Babylon) concludes with all heaven praising God's judgment with amens and alleluias. At this point in time (2007), the chances of finding any redemption in our degenerate West is virtually nil. The purpose of this book is to prepare people for World War III and the ensuing chaos.

St. John warns here that the attack will be sudden, unexpected and extremely widespread. He repeats the phrase "woe, woe" three times (18:10, 18:16, 18:19). A threefold repetition indicates the totality of the catastrophe. Why does the author say "woe, woe" when he had previously written "woe, woe, woe"? (8:13) The two "woes" make it clear that this section and chapter (R-9, Chapter 18) are still part of the second woe and verify the ROC arrangement as opposed to the standard text.

St. John also repeats the words "one hour" three times: "In one hour Babylon is made desolate" (18:19); "In one hour are so great riches come to naught" (18:17); and "In one hour is your judgment come." (18:10) It is difficult to interpret the start of the Great War as anything but a surprise nuclear attack.

After its short term of rule, Communism and the Antichrist's New World Tyranny will also be utterly destroyed, not by Capitalism, but by God's final chastisement. But first, in order to avoid God's punishment on decadent Capitalist countries through his chastising agent, Russia, Christians must take St. John's admonition of Chapter 18:4: "Go out from her my people." Does this mean building an "ark", finding a cave, or moving your family? There are two main weapons we can utilize in defeating the Antichrist: the offensive weapon is the Rosary; the defensive weapon is the Scapular. Beyond that, if you want to know what you must do personally, turn off your televisions, stop worshipping images of the beast, and God will tell you what to do! If you want to examine a group of religious people who have thoroughly exited Capitalism, study the Amish. The Amish are great candidates for rapture.

THE GREAT TRIBULATION

B-1 — FAMINE

*6:5   And when he had opened the third seal,
I heard the third living creature saying: come and see.
And behold a black horse, and he that sat on him
had a pair of scales in his hand.*

*6:6   And I heard as it were a voice in the midst of
the four living creatures, saying: Two pounds of wheat
for a penny, and thrice two pounds of barley for
a penny, and see you hurt not the wine and the oil.*

The third horseman (B-1), the Black Horse, famine, ushers in the Great Tribulation period. This represents the beginning of the reign of the eighth "Beast", World Tyranny, following the defeat of Capitalism (fall of Babylon). Famine, along with brutal persecution of Christians, will be the chief terrors of tyrannical world wide Socialist/Communist rule, just as it was after the Bolshevik revolution. The only consolation for Christians is to realize that Satan's time at running the planet will be shortened and all those who support him — the Antichrist, the False Prophet, the ten world leaders — will be violently cast into hell by divine retribution.

By restructuring St. John's text according to the ROC chart, we begin to see the big picture. Currently (2007), we are living through the Great Apostasy (W-1 — W-9). This era will be abruptly ended by the outbreak of World War III (R-1 — R-9) which will in turn be followed by the terrifying tribulation period (B-1 — B-9) which God will mercifully bring to a very sudden and unexpected end with the battle of Armagedon and the fiery chastising comet (P-1 — P-9).

B-2 — SEALED TRIBES OF ISRAEL

7:1   After these things I saw four angels standing on the four corners of the earth, holding the four winds of the earth, that they should not blow upon the earth, nor upon the sea, nor on any tree.

7:2   And I saw another angel ascending from the rising of the sun, having the seal of the living God: and he cried with a loud voice to the four angels, to whom it was given to hurt the earth and the sea.

7:3   Saying: Hurt not the earth, nor the sea, nor the trees, till we seal the servants of our God in their foreheads.

7:4   And I heard the number of them that were sealed, a hundred forty-four thousand sealed, of all the tribes of the children of Israel.

7:5   Of the tribe of Juda, twelve thousand sealed: of the tribe of Ruben, twelve thousand sealed: of the tribe of Gad, twelve thousand sealed:

7:6   Of the tribe of Aser, twelve thousand sealed: of the tribe of Naphtali, twelve thousand sealed: of the tribe of Manasses, twelve thousand sealed:

7:7   Of the tribe of Simeon, twelve thousand sealed: of the tribe of Levi, twelve thousand sealed: of the tribe of Issachar, twelve thousand sealed.

7:8   Of the tribe of Zabulon, twelve thousand sealed: of the tribe of Joseph, twelve thousand sealed: of the tribe of Benjamin, twelve thousand sealed.

Almighty God is planning to punish the punishers, the Communist One-World Tyranny that obliterates Capitalism. But the angels are told to refrain from their plagues on the Antichrist's kingdom until those who do not deserve punishment, the "servants of God", are sealed on their foreheads. This is a stark contrast to those who receive the mark of the Antichrist on their hands or foreheads and who thereby doom themselves to Hell.

The angel from the rising sun says "we" will seal the tribes of Israel. The "we" refers to the Two Witnesses Enoch and Elias who will appear on earth after the Great War and will convert many Jews in Israel. Although their deaths culminate in a remarkable resurrection, the Two Witnesses' return may be very unobtrusive and, in fact, they may be here already, along with their two antagonists, the Antichrist and the False Prophet.

The Great Tribulation   57

The "servants of God", as noted earlier, can represent several different kinds of martyrs, some of whom would absolutely avoid the sacrifice if they could, and they may not even be Christian. The 144,000 from the tribes of Israel and the countless "multitude" indicate another major holocaust during the Great Tribulation. The persecutions of Jews, and especially Jewish converts to Christ, and of Christians will make Stalin and Hitler look like amateurs.

The "earth", "sea" and "trees" that will be hurt after the tribes are sealed represent all segments of society (not the environment). Once the tribes are sealed, they also suffer the same punishments as the general population. The four winds — East, West, North and South — clearly imply a far reaching chastisement. Those who are sealed and not deserving the plagues will probably join the ranks of martyrs or perhaps be favored with later divine protection or rapture. Back in Chapter 9 (W-4), St. John uses almost identical phraseology describing the locusts of apostasy:

> 9:4   And it was commanded them that they should not hurt the grass of the earth, nor any green thing, nor any tree: but only the men who have not the sign of God on their foreheads.

Again the "green things" represent the faithful saints who avoid the "hurts" of heresy. But here the similarities end. The punishments of the earlier Great Apostasy are limited (the locusts cannot kill anyone) and the effects of the Protestant heresies are not, at least not yet, worldwide. In the original text, the lesser plagues in Chapter 9 follow the vision of impending complete destruction in Chapter 7. The ROC chart correctly places the greater punishments of the Great Tribulation in a later time frame than the lesser plagues of the Great Apostasy.

Most commentators note that no one from the tribe of Dan or Ephraim is mentioned as saved. St. John was himself a Jew and certainly omitted these tribes on purpose. Perhaps this is meant as a generalized warning from St. John to his fellow Jews that large groups of them will ultimately accept the Antichrist rather than Jesus as their Messiah.

> 7:9   After this I saw a great multitude, which no man could number, of all nations, and tribes, and peoples, and tongues: standing before the throne, and in the sight of the Lamb, clothed with white robes, and palms in their hands:
>
> 7:10   And they cried with a loud voice, saying:

Salvation to our God, who sits upon the throne, and to the Lamb.

7:11   And all the angels stood round about the throne, and about the ancients, and about the four living creatures: and they fell before the throne upon their faces, and adored God,

7:12   Saying: Amen. Benediction and glory, and wisdom, and thanksgiving, honor, and power, and strength to our God for ever and ever. Amen.

7:13   And one of the ancients answered and said to me: Who are these that are clothed in white robes, and whence are they come?

7:14   And I said to him: My lord, you know. And he said to me: these are they who are come out of great tribulation, and have washed their robes, and have made them white in the blood of the Lamb.

7:15   Therefore they are before the throne of God, and serve him day and night in his temple; and he that sits on the throne, shall dwell over them.

7:16   They shall not hunger nor thirst any more, neither shall the sun fall on them, nor any heat.

7:17   For the Lamb, which is in the midst of the throne, shall rule them, and shall lead them to the fountains of the waters of life, and God shall wipe away all tears from their eyes.

In Chapter 7:16, St. John mentions a trinity of tribulations which those in heaven no longer need endure: hunger, thirst, and heat. The hunger refers back to the Black Horse, Famine, which will come about not only from the destruction of much of the world's farm lands due to World War III, but also from the rationing instituted by the One World economic apparatus which will not allow any buying or selling without the "mark of the beast."

The thirst refers to the polluted waters which cover the planet, again from World War III, and will be experienced as "water turned to blood." During the Tribulation period, the Two Witnesses will also have the startling ability to turn water to "blood."

Finally, the "heat" and the "falling sun" refers to nuclear warfare and conventional weaponry. The dead who no longer suffer these plagues will be envied by the living. This trinity of plagues constitutes a land, sea and air type of trinity and thus a complete totality of destruction.

The bloodshed during the fierce reign of the godless New World

Disorder will be enormous. St. John says the martyrs will be a "great multitude which no man can number." To those who seek to avoid these trials, Jesus will say, "No servant is greater than his master." (Jn. 15:20) Christians be warned: if you take the mark of the Beast, it's true, you will avoid famine and martyrdom, but you will eventually be thrust into the lake of fire. This is the culmination of the Christian era and everyone must decide: will I accept the sign of the cross, join the sheep and die for the Lord? Or will I take the mark, join the goats who terrorize the sheep and end up in hell. This era in history is rightfully called "The Great Tribulation" and St. John uses that very term in 7:14.

B-3 — WORMWOOD

8:10   And the third angel sounded the trumpet, and a great star fell from heaven, burning as it were a torch, and it fell on the third part of the rivers, and upon the fountains of waters:

8:11   And the name of the star is called Wormwood. And the third part of the waters became wormwood; and many men died of the waters, because they were made bitter.

If the symbols St. John employs during the Great Apostasy describe spiritual trials and those during World War III physical trials, then the symbols he uses during the Great Tribulation (B-1 — B-9) can be either or both. The pain and suffering of famine and martyrdom is real, but then again so is the great sorrow of losing one's soul.

The star which burns like a torch is meant to give light rather than heat, and is the second great star to fall during the Apocalypse, the first being Martin Luther during the Apostasy. Here, the illumination from Wormwood is obscure because it represents an end-time antipope, the False Prophet who uses his authority over Catholics (one-third of the waters) to seduce them into supporting the Antichrist. They die a spiritual, not physical, death from his false doctrine (bitter waters). Eventually they die a violent physical death also and are thrust into hell along with the Antichrist, the False Prophet (Wormwood) and the rest of their followers.

The False Prophet is revealed here before the Antichrist because he will imitate the role of St. John the Baptist and announce the coming of the lawless one. There have been many other interpretations as to the identity of "Wormwood" from Satan to natural pollution to the barbarians who sacked Rome. Fr. Kramer comes closest by labeling

Wormwood a high ranking prelate, but then concludes he represents the Greek Schism.[8] Here is where the ROC chart is invaluable. If Fr. Kramer had realized that Wormwood comes onto the historical scene after WWIII but before the Antichrist, he would have easily seen that Wormwood can only be the False Prophet.

B-4 — TWO PROPHETS

10:1   And I saw another mighty angel come down from heaven clothed with a cloud, and a rainbow upon his head, and his face was as the sun, and his feet as pillars of fire:

10:2   And he had in his hand a little scroll, open: and he set his right foot upon the sea, and his left foot upon the land:

10:3   And he cried out with a loud voice, as when a lion roars. And when he had cried out, seven thunders uttered their voices.

10:4   And when the seven thunders had uttered their voices, I was about to write: and I heard a voice from heaven saying to me: Seal up the things which the seven thunders have spoken: and write them not.

10:5   And the angel, which I saw standing upon the sea, and upon the land, lifted up his hand to heaven:

10:6   And he swore by him that lives for ever and ever, who created heaven, and the things which are therein; and the earth, and the things which are therein; and the sea, and the things which are therein: That there shall be no more delay:

10:7   But that in the days of the voice of the seventh angel, when he shall begin to sound the trumpet, the mystery of God shall be finished, as he has declared by his servants, the prophets.

10:8 And I heard a voice from heaven speaking to me again, and saying: Go, and take the scroll, that is open, from the hand of the angel standing upon the sea, and upon the land.

10:9   And I went to the angel, saying unto him, that he should give me the scroll. And he said to me: Take the scroll and devour it: and it shall make your belly bitter, but in your mouth it shall be sweet as honey.

---

[8]Rev. Herman Bernard Kramer, *The Book of Destiny*, p. 203.

10:10   And I took the scroll from the hand of the angel, and devoured it: and it was in my mouth sweet as honey: and when I had devoured it, my belly was bitter:

10:11   And he said to me: you must prophesy again to nations, and peoples, and tongues, and to many kings.

Chapters 10 and 11 (B-4) depict several of the more important events which occur during the brutal reign of the "Beast from the abyss." The "mighty" angel which announces these events functions like another Trumpet Angel (he cries with a loud voice like a lion). He is the "eighth," albeit unnumbered Trumpet Angel between the sixth and seventh Trumpet Angels, and his purpose is to shout out a similar warning (seven thunders) except that the specifics of these warnings will remain hidden because St. John is instructed to "seal up" the messages.

The seven hidden "thunders" will ultimately be revealed, not to Christians, but to the followers of the Antichrist who will suffer through them. This will occur at the time of the seventh trumpet (P-4), which is part of the next series of nine events (P-1 — P-9), the Final Chastisement. How sure is the angel that "there shall be no more delay"? He swears by the land, sea and air which we immediately recognize as a perfect structural trinity and thus a reflection of God's power.

Why is the scroll describing these thunders "sweet" in the prophet's mouth but "bitter" in his belly? Because the final chastisement will be most welcome by Christians suffering the persecutions of the Antichrist's New World Tyranny but very bitter to his followers who must swallow and endure them. Christians will be instructed not to look out their windows at God's punishment on the evil ones, just as Lot and his family were told not to look back at the destruction of Sodom and Gomorrah.

Another reason these "thunders" are hidden from the reader's view is to prove that every other message in this Apocalypse is very pertinent indeed. Those who say these prophecies do not relate to them are fooling themselves. God is saying if you do not really need the prophecies in Revelation, He will keep them hidden just as the seven thunders are hidden. At this point, St. John himself believes that his public warnings are complete, but the angel tells him to continue prophesying. How important are these messages? They must be proclaimed to "many nations, and peoples, and tongues, and kings." (10:11)

11:1   And there was given me a reed like unto a rod, and it was said to me: Rise, and measure the temple of God, and the altar, and them that adore in it.

11:2   But the court, which is without the temple, cast out, and measure it not, because it is given to the Gentiles, and the holy city they shall tread under foot forty-two months:

11:3   And I will give to my two witnesses, and they shall prophesy a thousand two hundred sixty days, clothed in sackcloth.

11:4   These are the two olive-trees, and the two candlesticks, standing before the Lord of the earth.

11:5   And if any man would hurt them, fire shall come out of their mouths, and shall devour their enemies: and if any man would hurt them, in this manner must he be killed.

11:6   These have power to shut heaven, that it rain not in the days of their prophecy: and they have power over waters to turn them into blood, and to strike the earth with all plagues as often as they will.

11:7   And when they shall have finished their testimony, the beast, that ascends out of the abyss, shall make war against them, and shall overcome them, and kill them.

11:8   And their bodies shall lie in the streets of the great city, which spiritually is called Sodom, and Egypt, where also their Lord was crucified.

11:9   And they of the tribes, and peoples, and tongues, and nations, shall see their bodies for three days and a half: and shall not suffer their bodies to be laid in sepulchers.

11:10   And the inhabitants of the earth shall rejoice over them, and make merry: and shall send presents one to another, because these two prophets tormented them that dwelled upon the earth.

11:11   And after three days and a half, the spirit of life from God entered into them. And they stood upon their feet, and great fear fell upon them that saw them.

11:12   And they heard a great voice from heaven, saying to them: Come up hither. And they went up into heaven in a cloud: and their enemies saw them.

11:13   And at that hour there was a great earthquake, and the tenth part of the city fell: and there were slain in the earthquake, names of men seven thousand; and the rest were cast into a fear, and gave glory to the God of heaven.

11:14   The second woe is past: and behold the third woe will come quickly.

Next, St. John is told to "measure" the temple of God, but not the external court. This indicates schism. The true, faithful, remnant Christians will be those who worship at the altar, while all the external institutions of the Catholic Church — hospitals, schools, universities, orphanages, seminaries, convents, monasteries, houses of worship, etc. — will be taken over by the Antichrist, a trend which we are beginning to see already. Any Catholic hospital or university which dispenses contraceptives or hires abortionists has already capitulated to the enemy.

Contrary to popular exegesis, the Two Prophets are not slain by the Antichrist but rather by the New World Tyranny, the "Beast from the abyss." Since they prophesy in Jerusalem, the Israeli Government may not be at all pleased with their activities. In the past section St. John notes that 144,000 Jews are converted to Christ. Since they are Jewish themselves, Enoch and Elias will be very effective proselytizers.

Now Israel follows Italy into Communism and convinces the New World Disorder to bring its capital to Jerusalem, mostly in an attempt to silence the Two Witnesses. Even though he is not yet identified with the Antichrist, it's very possible that the "man of sin" will prove his credentials to be the "master of all evil" by killing the Witnesses where many others have failed. To clarify the above, the Beast from the abyss kills the Two Witnesses, but it may well be an anonymous Antichrist who pulls the trigger. Up until now, the Antichrist has been compelled to keep his identity hidden, but the wraps are off, and everyone will see his evil capabilities. Thus he is propelled onto the center of the world's stage and is recognized as the long awaited Antichrist of all time. There have been many restraints holding back the public appearance of the Antichrist. As St. Paul wrote, "You know what is restraining him now so that he may be revealed in time." (2 Thes. 2-6)

The Two Witnesses (B-4) also seem to indicate that the Pope and his hierarchy and all clergy will apostatize (or be martyred or be taken into hiding) because God will need to rely almost exclusively on the Two Witnesses as the last resort to reach His children. Since they prophesy 1260 days, that means they will survive until near the halfway point of the Tribulation which is also the beginning of the Antichrist's reign.

The ministry of these two "Olive Trees" undoubtedly begins about the same time as the appearance of Wormwood, the False Antipope. The Antipope and the two "Candlesticks" will work great signs and miracles countering each other in much the same way as Moses and the Pharaoh's magicians (Exodus 7).

Most analysts consider Enoch and Elijah to be the Two Witnesses who, according to the Old Testament, never died but were "translated." The Old Testament describes Elijah as being taken to

Heaven in a chariot of fire and that Enoch did not die but was taken away by God. The prophet Elijah will probably counter the False Prophet in all things spiritual. Enoch will serve as a foil in the temporal sphere to the "Beast from the abyss."

The powers these two "Candlesticks" manifest of stopping the rain and turning water to blood is very significant because fresh potable drinking water will be almost nonexistent. The One World Anti-system will be frustrated in gaining total control and allegiance from all humanity if the ability to provide the first and most basic need of all life is in the hands of the Two Prophets.

The world leaders, all of whom by this time are Communist (although they will avoid that term, preferring "One World" or "World Union" or some such platitudinous euphemism instead), send many assassins to kill the Two Prophets, but all fail, just as they failed to kill Pope John Paul II. At last, the worst of the world's dictators, the man who will assume the mantle of the Antichrist, will realize only he has the power to destroy God's witnesses and he goes to Jerusalem to confront them personally. When he succeeds, the whole world recognizes him as their (false) messiah.

The murder of these Two Witnesses solves the government's final problem and thus completes the second "woe" which began in R-2 with the surprise attack beginning World War III. They are the last organized opposition to the Evil World Empire and also the last martyrs to go to heaven! The total number of martyrs necessary to complete world history is now "filled up." Soon we will be introduced to a new category of martyrs envisioned by St. John whom he will call "blessed" which means they will return with Christ for the Millennium.

The next section (B-5) finally provides a concise picture of the two Beasts, the Antichrist and the False Prophet, although St. John has already referred to them several times. Now that the Two Witnesses are gone, the Two Beasts will be able to reveal themselves to the world in all their evility. The Two Witnesses preached for 1260 days. The Two Beasts rule for 42 months. Together they span the entire seven-year tribulation time period.

B-5 — TWO BEASTS

13:1   And I saw a beast coming out of the sea,
having seven heads and ten horns, and upon his horns
ten diadems, and upon his heads names of blasphemy.

13:2   And the beast which I saw was like to a
leopard, and his feet were as the feet of a bear, and

his mouth as the mouth of a lion. And the dragon gave him his own strength, and great power.

13:3   And I saw one of his heads as it were wounded to death: and his deadly wound was healed. And all the earth was in admiration after the beast.

13:4   And they adored the dragon, which gave power to the beast: and they adored the beast, saying: Who is like to the beast? and who shall be able to fight with it?

13:5   And there was given to it a mouth, speaking great things, and blasphemies: and power was given to it to act forty-two months.

13:6   And he opened his mouth in blasphemies against God, to blaspheme his name, and his tabernacle, and them that dwell in heaven.

13:7   And it was given to him to make war with the saints, and to overcome them: and power was given him over every tribe, and people, and tongue, and nation:

13:8   And all that dwell upon the earth adored him: whose names are not written in the book of life of the Lamb which was slain from the beginning of the world.

13:9   If any man have an ear, let him hear.

13:10   He that shall lead into captivity, shall go into captivity: he that shall kill by the sword, must be killed by the sword. Here is the patience and the faith of the saints.

Sections B-4 and B-5 are another paired grouping that gives credence to the new ROC text reordering. B-4 describes in detail the Two Witnesses who stand up to the One World Tyranny and B-5 describes in detail the two principle villains of this evil establishment, the Antichrist and the False Prophet (Antipope) who wage war against the Two Witnesses and eventually kill them. This marks the second great turning point in Revelation. When the second woe ends, the greatest secret of the secret societies, the identity of the Antichrist is revealed. Also, the Pope and his remnant Church go into hiding, the Raptured are removed from earth, the headquarters of the Beast moves to Jerusalem and the fierce tyranny of the Antichrist engulfs the planet.

Following the murder of Enoch and Elias by the New World Conspiracy, the Antichrist will be free to reveal himself and initiate his forty-two month reign as World Dictator. The "Beast" coming up out of the sea here with seven heads and ten horns is **not** the same as the World

Totalitarian Government which will defeat decadent Capitalism and move its headquarters from Moscow to Rome. The seven heads of that Beast represent seven great world tyrannies culminating in Socialist/Communism which will become the "eighth Beast." The ten heads of that Beast will be the Ten Nation Confederation (basically the European Union) which will hand over their sovereignty and their Capital, Rome, to World Tyranny.

This new "Beast" from the sea is the Antichrist in person. Fr. Kramer in his work, "The Book Of Destiny," suggests that the "sea" means the Mediterranean Sea and this Man of Sin will come from some country which borders that body of water. He will be Jewish, but since he's from the lost tribe of Dan, his heritage may not be apparent even to himself. He is the personification of the eighth World Beast and its phony leader. His "ten horns" refers to all the world leaders who are subservient to him and who undoubtedly select him from their ranks to be their "fuehrer." The diadems upon their horns indicate their positions of authority in their individual nations or regions of the world and they all will be cast into hell along with the Antichrist, the Antipope and Satan.

The seven heads of the Beast have "names of blasphemy." This implies that they are the heads of the world's false religions. Both the numbers "ten" and "seven" are symbolic numbers and therefore approximate. Since St. John writes that the Antichrist will have power over "every tribe, and people, and tongue, and nation," in fact **all** the world's political and religious leaders will support this New World Tyrant.

The only exception will be our next (and last) Pope, Peter II. Our current (and next to last Pope), Benedict XVI (who is called the "glory of the olive" by St. Malachy), will apparently be martyred (according to the third secret of Fatima- see appendix B) and will be replaced by an Antipope called "Wormwood" by St. John. Benedict's legitimate successor, the true Pope, Peter II, will be forced into hiding, as indicated in W-5 when the Woman (Mary) and her remnant "seed" (spiritual children) flee to a desert place for protection.

Our next Pope may not only be hidden, he may be practically unknown since Pope Benedict XVI's illegally selected successor, the False Prophet, will control the entire apparatus of the Catholic Church from St. Peter's Basilica in Rome down to every Catholic school, university, church, hospital, seminary, convent, etc. which, as revealed in B-4, will be "trodden under by the Gentiles." Truly, the Church will be crucified just like her bridegroom, Jesus our Messiah!

The first task for the Antichrist in his new world capital, Jerusalem, will be to try and restore the prestige of the One World Tyranny after it finally succeeds in assassinating the Two Witnesses only to see them resurrected, probably in full view of television cameras, and visibly taken up to heaven.

First, he may claim that the resurrection was a case of UFO alien abduction, which the millions of readers of supermarket tabloids will readily accept. But to show that he can also resurrect people, he and possibly some of the world religious leaders will concoct an elaborate deception. One of them, that is one of Antichrist's blasphemous heads, will feign to be killed and the Antichrist will bring him back to life. St. John emphasizes that this will be a phony miracle because the religious leader will only appear to be slain, "as it were." Not just tabloids, but also the mainstream media will buy into this lie and proclaim the Antichrist to be a God.

Practically all interpreters of Revelation claim that the Antichrist suffers the "head" wound himself and pretends a resurrection in imitation of Christ. It could happen this way, but the most important thing to remember is that the "miracle" is phony and that the "healing" occurs after the true resurrection of the Two Witnesses and is a pathetic response to that Godly miracle.

The leader of the One World Religion will be the False Pope who will also undoubtedly be elected head of the World Council of Churches and similar organizations. After he announces Antichrist's coming, he will follow him and move the Vatican to Jerusalem. It is from Jerusalem that these two evildoers enforce the tyrannical laws outlined in verses 12-17.

The word "Beast" can refer to both the One World Empire as well as its principal architect, the Antichrist, just as the "woman clothed with the sun" represents both Mary and her spiritual seed, the Church. The fierce animalistic character of the Antichrist — bear, lion and leopard — contrasts with the heavenly jewels which grace our Lady — the sun, moon and stars.

> *13:11   And I saw another beast coming up out of the earth, and he had two horns, like to a lamb's, and he spoke as a dragon.*
>
> *13:12   And he executed all the power of the former beast in his sight: and he caused the earth, and them that dwell therein, to adore the first beast, whose deadly wound was healed.*
>
> *13:13   And he did great signs, so that he made even fire to come down from heaven upon the earth in the sight of man.*
>
> *13:14   And he seduced them that dwell on the earth, by the signs, which were given him to perform in the*

sight of the beast, saying to them that dwell on the earth, that they should make an image to the beast, which had the wound by the sword, and lived.

13:15   And it was given him to give life to the image of the beast, and that the image of the beast should speak: and should cause, that whoever will not adore the image of the beast, should be slain.

13:16   And he shall make all, both little and great, rich and poor, freemen and bondmen, to have a mark in their right hand, or in their foreheads.

13:17   And that no man might buy or sell, but he that has the mark, or the name of the beast, or the number of his name.

13:18   Here is wisdom. He that has understanding, let him compute the number of the beast. For it is the number of a man: and his number is six hundred sixty-six.

The Antichrist (World Leader) and the Antipope (False Prophet) will put on a great show of being meek as lambs but are in reality as ravenous as wolves. Life under the eighth World Tyrannical Order will be the worst ever. It will be hell on earth.

The second Beast coming up out of the earth represents the False Prophet or Antipope. Fr. Kramer states that the "earth" that he comes from represents the "gentiles."[9] This indicates, by contrast, that the Antichrist is a Jew, probably from the tribe of Dan, which is excluded from St. John's list of the tribes of Israel from which 144,000 are saved. The gentile False Prophet (The Antipope) will exercise his chief function by promoting a false One World Religion organized to worship the Antichrist.

The three rulers in Rome plus Satan constitute the four evil entities of Revelation: the Dragon (Satan), the One World Beast, the Antichrist, and the False Prophet (Antipope). As is becoming readily apparent, the numbers "three" and "four" are very significant in St. John's work, and the four evil entities can be subdivided into three separate groupings of three each. The three "Beasts" are the Antichrist, the World Beast, and the False Prophet. The three who "go to hell" are the False Prophet, Satan and the Antichrist. The three with "seven heads and ten horns" are the Dragon, the World Beast and the Antichrist.

The three evil entities who "go to hell," as expressed by St. John, form an unholy trinity which parodies the true Holy Trinity. The

---

[9]Rev. H. B. Kramer, *The Book of Destiny*, p. 318. Fr. Kramer's descriptions of the two beasts are extensive and very insightful.

Dragon (Satan) from the air, the seven-headed Beast (Antichrist) from the sea, and the two horned Beast (False Prophet, or Antipope) from the earth form a structural trinity (solid, liquid, and gas). When all three parts of a structural trinity are present, that means the evil is unified, total and complete. Each one of the four evil entities has seven main attributes or activities for a total of twenty-eight. (It should be noted that "Babylon" sells twenty-eight different kinds of merchandise which are described by the author in groupings of three and four (18:12-16).

DRAGON FROM AIR

12:3	Has seven heads and ten horns
12:4	Tail drags one third of stars from sky
12:7	Battles St. Michael and is cast to earth
12:13	Persecutes the Woman
12:15	Casts river after woman
12:17	Makes war with the Woman's seed
12:18	Stands upon sand of the sea

BEAST FROM ABYSS

16:10	Kingdom becomes dark
17:3	Has seven heads and ten horns
17:3	Is full of blasphemy
17:8	Was, is not, goes to destruction
17-13	Receives power from ten kings
17-16	Will make harlot desolate
11-7	Kills Two Prophets

BEAST FROM SEA

13:1	Has seven heads and ten horns
13:2	Receives power from the Dragon
13:2	Features of lion, bear, leopard
13:3	Head wound is healed
13:5	Receives power for forty-two months
13:6	Blasphemes God and His tabernacle
13:7	Overcomes saints, gains power over entire earth

BEAST FROM EARTH

13:11	Has two horns like lamb, speaks like dragon
13:12	Executes power of first beast
13:12	Causes earth to adore Beast

13:13   Causes fire to come down from heaven

13:14   Forces everyone to adore image of Beast

13:15   Causes image of Beast to speak

13:16   Forces everyone to take mark of Beast

Another series of four occurrences which are actually a combination of two groups consisting of three events in one group and one in the other are the 1260 day time periods which refer to four different events, three of which occur simultaneously. The one isolated occurrence is the 1260 days that the Two Witnesses prophesy during the first half of the seven years of tribulation (B-4). The second half of the seven years of tribulation is marked by three coinciding events: the forty-two month reign of Antichrist, the 1260 days that the "Woman" is nourished in the desert (W-5 and R-5) and the forty-two months that the holy city is "trodden under foot by the Gentiles." (B-4) The "holy city" stands for Jerusalem "trodden" by the Antichrist as well as the Catholic church "trodden" by the Antipope.

There has always been much speculation as to what the "image of the beast" consists of and what is meant by "worshipping the Beast." The technology is already available for televised images to be transmitted world wide and also for cameras to be installed inside video receivers to send pictures of anyone watching back to those in charge of monitoring TV signals to determine if someone may not be giving a "seig heil" every time the Antichrist's image is flashed on the screen. It's hard to believe that in the twenty-first century we could go back to emperor worship, but the black horse of "famine" will be an overwhelming incentive to facilitate the enslaving of the entire population of earth.

B-6 — MARK OF THE BEAST

14:9   And the third angel followed them, saying with a loud voice: If any man shall adore the beast and his image, and receive his mark in his forehead, or in his hand;

14:10   He also shall drink of the wine of the wrath of God, which is mingled with pure wine in the cup of his wrath, and shall be tormented with fire and brimstone in the sight of the holy angels and in the sight of the Lamb.

14:11   And the smoke of their torments shall ascend up for ever and ever: neither have they rest day nor night, who have adored the beast, and his image, and whoever receives the mark of his name.

14:12   Here is the patience of the saints, who keep the commandments of God, and the faith of Jesus.

14:13   And I heard a voice from heaven, saying to me: Write: Blessed are the dead, who die in the Lord. From henceforth now, said the spirit, that they may rest from their labors; for their works follow them.

The previous segment of the tribulation period ended with "the second woe is past." (11:14) This next tribulation period (B-5 — P-2) could be called the "woe between woes" — that is, between the second woe, World War III, and the third woe, divine chastisement. It's evident that St. John considers the first half of the reign of the Antichrist as a continuation of World War III. When mankind actually passes through these stages of the Apocalypse, there may not be any sharp historical delineation.

The third Herald Angel once again recounts the choice Christians face under the Antichrist: either knuckle under, take the mark, lose your freedom in order to avoid famine, or risk your life by following Christ. A third option of taking up arms against the Evil Tyranny just isn't possible for those espousing true Christianity. Today's persuasive media personalities who claim that hoarding gold or hiding guns is the answer are lying! Why is God's punishment so great for adoring the Beast and his image? Because it violates the very First Commandment, "Thou shalt not have false Gods before me."

Looking ahead several chapters, after the battle of Armagedon, the Lord institutes a thousand-year reign for the saints with Christ on earth. This may be referred to as the Millennium or sometimes as the marriage feast of the Lamb. However, not everyone who has died during the apocalyptic time period will be eligible for this stupendous honor. Even the martyrs who died for the faith during the Great Apostasy or during World War III, or even during the first half of the Tribulation, will not qualify.

But at some point during this great tribulation time frame, those who are martyred will begin to be chosen for their eventual return to life on a renewed earth. That point starts when the "voice from heaven" declares in 14:13 that "henceforth" the dead are blessed. All previous martyrs, up to and including the Two Witnesses, went to heaven. Now it will take such a superhuman effort to accept martyrdom that the reward will be the thousand year reign on earth with Christ. (The word "blessed" appears in B-6, B-8, and B-9 and refers to the three favored groups who will reign with Christ: the Martyred, the Raptured, and the Protected.)

Perhaps the true end-time Pope, Peter II, will preach as a dogma that those who die at the hands of the Antichrist will gain this millennial privilege. Because every Pope since Peter obtains the "keys to the kingdom," he could proclaim this blessing a dogma and it would be as binding in heaven as it is on earth.

The Pope may find no other resort than such a dogma because all resistance to the New World Tyranny and the New World Religion has evaporated. The Antichrist's beheadings and torture of Christians is so cruel, that the courage of the faithful can only be buoyed up by the hope of a Millennium reward in order for them to be willing to accept the most barbaric of martyrdoms.

B-7 — RIVERS MADE BLOOD

16:4   And the third poured out his bowl upon the rivers and the fountains of waters; and there was made blood.

16:5   And I heard the angel of the waters saying: you are just, O Lord, who are, and who was, the Holy One because you have judged these things:

16:6   For they have shed the blood of the saints and prophets, and you have given them blood to drink; for they are worthy.

16:7   And I heard another, from the altar, saying: Yes, O Lord God Almighty, true and just are your judgments.

The symbols St. John uses to describe happenings during the great tribulation period continue to express both real and spiritual trials. Just as there is famine, the water also will be contaminated during the reign of the Beast. Rearranging the text clarifies what is meant here by the rivers and fountains turning to blood. In the original sequence, this event immediately follows paragraph 3 in R-7, "And the second angel poured out his bowl upon the sea and there came blood as it were a dead man." If you relied on the original sequence, you would not be remiss to consider that the two events are almost identical, whereas in fact, they are very different.

In the case of "dead man's blood," the blood is real blood and comes from bodies killed by the nuclear attack of World War III which decay and putrefy the water. In this second case, the water turned to "blood" is a heaven-sent plague visited upon the One World Tyranny of the Antichrist which is undoubtedly the same as the power of the Two Witnesses as described in R-4: "They have power over the waters to turn them to blood." This is very unlikely real blood but a form of pollution which certainly renders the water undrinkable.

B-8 — ANTICHRIST GATHERS ARMY

16:13   And I saw from the mouth of the dragon, and from the mouth of the beast, and from the mouth of the false prophet, three unclean spirits like frogs.

16:14   For they are the spirits of devils working signs, and they go forth unto the kings of the whole earth, to gather them to battle against the great day of Almighty God.

16:16   And he shall gather them together into a place, which in Hebrew is called Armagedon.

16:15   Behold, I come as a thief. Blessed is he that watches, and keeps his garments, lest he walk naked and they see his shame.

Satan, the Antichrist, and the False Pope realize their days are numbered and they manipulate all the world's rulers through miraculous signs to join their final conflict with the Lamb. Armagedon refers to the area around the town of Megiddo approximately 50 miles north of Jerusalem. St. John again warns Christians not to be deceived. The battle on the plains of Megiddo is both physical and spiritual, and will occur near the end of the third woe, which is Divine Chastisement.

The three frogs symbolize the lies and propaganda spouted by the unholy trio. Using today's terminology, they are the "willing accomplices of the drive-by media." Their agenda is not peace and harmony, which generates only meek, mild, and nonviolent headlines, but rather total disruption of society to the point of obliterating all that is good and holy. Although their goal is "order out of chaos," first they must create the turmoil and chaos. Other "spirits and devils working signs" can already be observed today in "UFO's," "crop circles," "animal mutilations," "big foot phenomena" and other manifestations of demonic activity which will only get worse as the New World Disorder develops.

Here in B-8, St. John describes the second group who are "blessed": those who "watch and keep their garments clean." Although they receive this unique grace, no mention is made that they are martyrs or in heaven (like the first "blessed" in B-6). Rather, these are the "protected," Mary's "seed" (spiritual children) who flee to a safe desert place and survive into the thousand year era of peace.

B-9 — CHRIST GATHERS ARMY

19:5   And a voice came out from the throne, saying: Praise you our God all his servants: and you that fear him, little and great.

19:6   And I heard as it were the voice of a great multitude, and as the voice of many waters, and as the voice of great thunders, saying: Alleluia: for the Lord our God, the omnipotent, has reigned.

19:7   Let us be glad and rejoice: and give glory to him: for the marriage of the Lamb is come, and his wife has prepared herself.

19:8   And to her it has been granted, that she should clothe herself with fine linen, glittering and white. For the fine linen are the justifications of saints.

19:9   And he said to me: Write: Blessed are they who are called to the marriage supper of the Lamb: and he said to me: These words of God are true.

19:10   And I fell down before his feet, to adore him, and he said to me

See you do it not: I am your fellow-servant, and of your brethren who have the testimony of Jesus. Adore God. For the testimony of Jesus is the spirit of prophecy.

19:11   And I saw heaven opened, and behold a white horse; and he that sat upon him, was called Faithful and True, and with justice he judges and fights.

19:12   And his eyes were as a flame of fire, and on his head many diadems, having a name written, which no man knows but himself.

19:13   And he was clothed with a garment sprinkled with blood: and his name is called, THE WORD OF GOD.

19:14   And the armies which are in heaven followed him on white horses, clothed in fine linen, white and clean.

*19:15   And out of his mouth proceeds a sharp
two-edged sword: that with it he may strike
the Gentiles. And he shall rule them with a rod
of iron: and he treads the wine press of the
fury of the wrath of God the Almighty.*

*19:16   And he has on his garment and on his
thigh written: King of kings, and Lord of lords.*

Sections B-8 and B-9 reveal another set of paired events which follow one another and serve to verify the ROC text arrangement. The obvious close relationship between these two particular occurrences is hidden in the original text because they are separated by three chapters.

B-8 describes Satan, the Antichrist, and the False Prophet preparing for Armagedon. They convince the rest of the world to join them by spouting propaganda and "unclean spirits like frogs" issue from their mouths (media outlets). Following their defeat of the Church and murder of the Two Witnesses, the unholy trio need only to defeat Christ and his faithful armies to claim victory on earth, Satan's goal ever since he was cast out of heaven.

In section B-9, Christ the Lamb in His turn prepares for Armagedon. He gathers His heavenly army and out of His mouth proceeds "a sharp, two-edged sword." Christ's army of the Raptured is awesome, and, whereas the decadent forces of Babylon (Capitalism) could not defeat the Beast (One World Tyranny), the Evil Beast and the Unholy Trio are no match for the Son of God.

The "marriage supper of the Lamb" (19:9) refers to the Millennium which concludes the battle about to take place. Those who are called to this feast are once again labeled special and unique; St. John calls them "blessed." Like the Protected, no comment is made that they will stay in heaven wearing white robes and playing harps or that they are martyrs. Instead these are the saints who are Raptured and who will "follow" the Lamb. They will be seen again in P-5 returning with Christ on Mt. Sion.

THE GREAT CHASTISEMENT

P-1 — PALE HORSE — DEATH

6:7   And when he had opened the fourth seal,
I heard the voice of the fourth living creature saying:
come, and see.

6:8   And behold a pale horse, and he that sat
upon him, his name was Death, and hell followed him.
And power was given to him over the four parts of the
earth, to kill with sword, with famine, and with death,
and with the beasts of the earth.

The fourth (P-1), pale colored horse, carries the rider "death" which is the hallmark of the One World Tyranny. Death is also what God will mete out to the Antichrist, the False Prophet and their followers. Some people suggest that the Antichrist will even revive feeding Christians to the lions. If you want to know what life will be like under this New World Order, just read Aleksandr Solzhenitsyn's *Gulag Archipelago.*

The third woe, divine chastisement, is referred to by St. Jacinta as the "secret of heaven." Just as the faithful rejoiced over the fall of godless Capitalism, how much more joy will they feel when they realize that God's hand is about to fall on the last Beast?

P-2 — SILENCE IN HEAVEN

8:1   And when he had opened the seventh seal,
there was silence in heaven, as it were for half an
hour.

8:2   And I saw seven angels standing in the
presence of God; and there were given to them seven
trumpets.

> *8:3   And another angel came, and stood before*
> *the altar, having a golden censer; and there was given*
> *to him much incense, that he should offer of the*
> *prayers of all saints upon the golden altar, which is*
> *before the throne of God.*
>
> *8:4   And the smoke of the incense of the prayers*
> *of the saints ascended up before God from the hand of*
> *the angel.*
>
> *8:5   And the angel took the censer, and filled it*
> *with fire of the altar, and cast it on the earth, and*
> *there were thunders and voices and lightnings, and a*
> *great earthquake.*

Christ opens the seventh seal and we see the calm before the storm. God is about to answer the prayers of the martyrs after the opening of the earlier fifth seal: "How long, O Lord, do you not judge and avenge our blood." They no longer have to "rest for a little time." Vengeance is mine, says the Lord. (Rom. 12:19)

The silence also refers to a cessation of prophetic warnings from the Blessed Mother to the children of earth. Public messages to mankind will dry up as God throws up His hands and throws in the towel. If people insist on trying to exist free from God and enslaved to the Antichrist, let them have their "half hour" of utter hedonism and hopelessness. Since the Antichrist's only answer to the problems of a society without God will be to blame and execute Christians, he will follow the historical precedence from Nero to Waco.

The "fire" cast down from heaven is a comet which collides with earth. The spinning "sun" which plunged to earth at Fatima was a preview of this catastrophe. The comet causes disruptions in the earth's atmosphere while the "voices" are those of demons who will taunt the terrified adorers of Antichrist.

P-3 — DARKENED SUN

> *8:12   And the fourth angel sounded the trumpet,*
> *and the third part of the sun was smitten, and the third*
> *part of the moon, and the third part of the stars, so*
> *that the third part of them was darkened, and the day*
> *did not shine for a third part of it, and the night in*
> *like manner.*

Debris from the comet darkens the sun, moon and stars, possibly precipitated by a preliminary fly-by of the comet on its path to orbit the sun. This chastising comet is the third "woe" and will come upon mankind very suddenly. The smug kingdom of the Antichrist will most likely be panic-stricken.

P-4 — EARTHQUAKE AND HAIL

11:15   And the seventh angel sounded the trumpet; and there were great voices in heaven, saying: the kingdom of this world is become our Lord's and his Christ's, and he shall reign for ever and ever. Amen.

11:16   And the four and twenty ancients, who sit on their seats in the sight of God fell on their faces and adored God, saying:

11:17   We give you thanks, O Lord God Almighty, who are, and who was, and who is to come: because you have taken to yourself great power, and you have reigned.

11:18   And the nations were angry, and your wrath is come, and the time of the dead, that they should be judged, and that you should render reward to your servants the prophets and the saints, and to them that fear your name, little and great, and should destroy them who have corrupted the earth.

11:19   And the temple of God was opened in heaven; and the ark of his testament was seen in his temple, and there were lightnings, and voices, and an earthquake, and great hail.

God's power and majesty is becoming increasingly apparent to the New World Tyranny as the comet approaches earth probably after orbiting the sun. The "nations are angry" that the good will be rewarded, meaning those they have killed or incarcerated, while those who corrupted the earth — the Antichrist and his followers — will be destroyed. The "great hail" is more debris from the comet.

This section from Chapter 11 is a good example of the efficacy of the new ROC text rearrangement. This judgment clearly belongs near the chronological end of the apocalyptic period, not back at the one-third mark. In Chapter 10, this seventh trumpet is previewed and St. John writes, "But in the days of the seventh angel, when he shall begin to sound the trumpet, the mystery of God shall be finished." This last "mystery of God" refers to the phenomenon that will occur at this very end of the Antichrist's reign: the secret plagues of the seven thunders, which were sealed up back in Chapter 10, will be opened.

When will the seven thunders actually be revealed? "When the temple of God was opened in heaven and the ark of his testament was seen in his temple." The first time (Chapter 15) the "temple of the tabernacle of the testimony in heaven was opened" (almost the exact same phraseology), the seven angels with the bowls of the seven last plagues were released. Here the reader must put two and two together: seven plagues will be released here also, except that they are secret plagues from the hand of God, too horrible to describe, the plagues of the seven thunders, the plagues which will affect the followers of the Antichrist and his One World Tyranny but not the faithful believers. Doubtless, these plagues involve demons, the "voices" mentioned in 11:19.

P-5 — 144,000 SAVED VIRGINS

14:1   And I saw: and behold a Lamb stood on Mount Sion, and with him a hundred forty-four thousand having his name, and the name of his Father, written in their foreheads.

14:2   And I heard a voice from heaven, as the voice of many waters, and as the voice of great thunder: and the voice which I heard, was as of harpers, harping on their harps.

14:3   And they sung as it were a new canticle, before the throne, and before the four living creatures, and the ancients, and no man could say the canticle, but those hundred forty-four thousand, who were purchased from the earth.

14:4   These are they who were not defiled with women: for they are virgins. These follow the Lamb wherever he goes. These were purchased from among men, the first fruits to God, and to the Lamb:

14:5   And in their mouth was found no lie: for they are without spot before the throne of God.

Who are these 144,000 virgins? They are unique in four respects:
* They sing a "new" canticle which no other man can say;
* They are "not defiled with women" — an unusual grace in these latter days
* Though highly favored, there is no indication they have been martyred.
* They follow the "Lamb" wherever He goes.

That they tell no lies or have the name of the Father written on their foreheads is not so unique, but of all the groups previously mentioned, they are the only ones to stand with the Lamb on Mt. Sion (Zion). In fact, they have been chosen to return with the Lord to set up His reign during the Millennium. They are the "armies", as depicted back in B-9, who will fight against the Antichrist and his followers at Armagedon in P-9. Therefore these are the fortunate believers who were raptured out of the tribulation period in B-9. (More on the Martyred, Raptured and Protected later.)

P-6 — GRIM REAPER

14:14   And I saw, and behold a white cloud: and upon the cloud one sitting like to the Son of man, having on his head a golden crown, and in his hand a sharp sickle.

14:15   And another angel came out of the temple, crying with a loud voice to him that sat upon the cloud: Thrust in your sickle, and reap, because the hour is come to reap, for the harvest of the earth is ripe.

14:16   And he that sat on the cloud, put his sickle to the earth, and the earth was reaped.

14:17   And another angel came out of the temple, which is in heaven, he also having a sharp sickle.

14:18   And another angel came out from the altar, who had power over fire: and he cried with a loud voice to him that had the sharp sickle, saying: Thrust in your sharp sickle, and gather the clusters of the vineyard of the earth: because the grapes thereof are ripe.

14:19   And the angel put his sharp sickle to the earth, and gathered the vineyard of the earth, and cast it into the great press of the wrath of God.

14:20   And the press was trodden without the city, and the blood came out of the press up to the horses bridles, for a thousand and six hundred furlongs.

The fourth herald angel announces the "harvest is ripe." It's becoming clear why the fourth horseman, the "pale rider," is labeled "death." (P-1) The image of the grim reaper harvesting the "grapes" is a universal symbol of actual, physical death and the blood is real. All the previous world tyrannical empires have been destroyed. Now the eighth Beast, the final government without God, will be obliterated directly by the hand of God. Here is another passage from the middle of Revelation (Chapter 14) which obviously belongs near the end. This image is repeated in Chapter 19: "He treads the winepress of the fierceness of the wrath of God the almighty."

P-7 — SUN SCORCHES

16:8   And the fourth angel poured out his bowl upon the sun, and it was given to him to afflict men with heat and fire:

16:9   And men were scorched with great heat, and they blasphemed the name of God, who has power over these plagues, neither did they penance to give him glory.

The "sun" in this passage is the chastising comet which scorches the earth before colliding with it. Notice that no mention is made of the remnant Christians and their reaction to this disaster. By this time all will have been either martyred, incarcerated in "reeducation" camps, raptured, or sequestered away with the Blessed Mother in a safe place (W-8).

Also, note that despite the impending disaster of planetary collision, the followers of Antichrist refuse to repent. Clearly, in the Apocalypse, St. John is relating the culmination of human history. The sheep have truly been separated from the goats. There is no middle ground. Those who are not worthy to set up Christ's kingdom on earth will be removed in this Great Chastisement.

P-8 — GREAT CITY DIVIDED

16:17   And the seventh angel poured out his bowl into the air, and a great voice came out of the temple from the throne, saying: It is done.

16:18   And there were lightnings, and voices, and thunders, and there was a great earthquake, such as never has been since men were upon the earth: such an earthquake, so great.

16:19   And the great city was made into three parts: and the cities of the Gentiles fell, and great Babylon came in remembrance before God, to give to her the cup of the wine of the indignation of his wrath.

16:20   And every island fled away, and the mountains were not found.

16:21   And great hail like a talent came down from heaven upon men: and men blasphemed God for the plague of the hail; because it was exceedingly great.

The greatest earthquake (P-8) in mankind's history is caused by the comet colliding with earth. The "hail" which weighs hundreds of pounds is not ordinary bits of ice but rather pieces which break off from the comet. Even what is left of Babylon, which became a habitation for demons following World War III, will feel the effects of this final destruction. This is yet another passage that must be positioned just preceding the concluding chapters 19 and 20. The phrase "it is done" means we are talking about the very end. In the traditional sequence, this section, chapter 16, comes ahead of the fall of Babylon, chapter 17, which was engineered by the Beast from the abyss. But these last nine sections headed by the Pale Horse (P-1 — P-9) relate the New World Disorder's downfall. The defeat of the Beast cannot precede its victory over Babylon.

P-9 — FINAL VICTORY

19:17   And I saw an angel, standing in the sun, and he cried with a loud voice, saying to all the birds that did fly through the midst of heaven: Come, and gather yourselves together to the great supper of God,

19:18   That you may eat the flesh of kings, and the flesh of tribunes, and the flesh of mighty men, and the flesh of horses, and of them that sit on them, and the flesh of all freemen, and bondmen, and of little and great.

19:19   And I saw the beast, and the kings of the earth and their armies gathered together, to make war with him that sat upon the horse, and with his army.

19:20   And the beast was taken, and with him the false prophet: who wrought signs before him, wherewith he seduced them, who received the mark of the beast, and who adored his image. These two were cast alive into the pool of fire burning with brimstone.

19:21   And the rest were slain by the sword of him that sits upon the horse, which proceeds out of his mouth; and all the birds were filled with their flesh.

Chapters 19:17-21 and Chapter 20 (P-9) are celebrations of Christ's defeat of the eighth Beast and the kings of earth and His prior judgment of Babylon. The only life left after the chastising comet strikes earth seems to be birds which make a feast on the carrion of millions, perhaps billions of bodies. Images of this defeat of the Antichrist can be found in Ezechiel 38 and 39.

The destruction of the Antichrist's One World Antisystem comes directly from the hand of God (the chastising comet). In Section B-8, we see Satan, the Antichrist, and the False Pope recruit the world's leaders and "gather them together into a place, which in Hebrew is called Armagedon." The "sun" which the angel "stands in" represents the chastising comet.

Evidently, the Antichrist, seeing the end is near, believes he can prevent the calamity by attacking Christ and his followers. Or, he may simply decide he wants to cause as much destruction as possible before the inevitable. This final battle, and its conclusion, is described in only two brief paragraphs, 19:19 and 19:20. St. Jacinta calls this battle the "secret of heaven." Compare St. John's description of this final battle to his voluminous coverage of the defeat of Babylon (Capitalism) in World War III.

This is a further indication that however terrible the consequences of Armagedon will be for the unholy trio and their supporters, the details must remain a secret. God unleashes the "seven thunders" that the angel told St. John to "seal up" (10:4), but the faithful must get out of the way, shield their eyes, find enclosed seclusion, and avoid any contact with this cataclysmic divine punishment.

> *20:1   And I saw an angel coming down from heaven, having the key of the bottomless pit, and a great chain in his hand.*
>
> *20:2   And he laid hold on the dragon, the old serpent, which is the devil and satan, and bound him for a thousand years:*
>
> *20:3   And he cast him into the bottomless pit, and shut him up, and set a seal upon him, that he should no more seduce the nations, till the thousand years be finished: and after that, he must be loosed a little time.*
>
> *20:4   And I saw seats, and they sat upon them: and judgment was given unto them: and the souls of them that were beheaded for the testimony of Jesus, and for the word of God, and who had not adored the beast, nor his image, nor received his mark in their foreheads, or in their hands, and they lived and reigned with Christ a thousand years.*
>
> *20:5   The rest of the dead lived not till the thousand years were finished. This is the first resurrection.*

20:6   Blessed and holy is he that has part in the
first resurrection: in these the second death has no
power: but they shall be priests of God and of Christ,
and shall reign with him a thousand years.

Christians should become aware that there are only five possible conclusions to their lives in these end times. They may die a natural death before being required to take the mark of the Beast. They may apostatize, take the mark, and ultimately fall into hell. They may be fortunate enough to be raptured. They may become "Mary's seed," her spiritual children, and find safe haven in the "desert" protected for her. Or they may be beheaded as martyrs for refusing the mark. Only the last three categories will join Christ in the ensuing thousand-year reign of peace. It's especially important to note that those who are protected or raptured have no advantage over those who are martyred.

This thousand-year reign of the faithful who have successfully passed the "final exam," and who join with their bridegroom, Jesus Christ, is called the Millennium, and the "marriage supper" by St. John. This marriage feast is alluded to in the gospels in Jesus' parable about the five wise and five foolish virgins. The five wise virgins are prepared for the feast by keeping oil in their lamps, while the five foolish virgins are cast outside.

All the trials, tribulations, trumpets, seals and bowls of the apocalyptic end-times are tests to discover who is worthy to enter into the millennial reign with Christ. Although the task is more difficult than that experienced by any previous generation, the reward is also exceptional. No previous generation is eligible for the Millennium. No previous generation has even been allowed to take the final exam.

The Millennium is not some "pie in the sky" pipe dream, but the focal point for the entire book of Revelation. This is what we pray for when we say, "Thy kingdom come, thy will be done on earth as it is in heaven." The two wars, Babylon vs the Beast and the Beast vs the Lamb (Armagedon), tell how Christ will destroy the two unworthy economic, political and social systems of our times, Capitalism and Communism. The decadent thesis and the godless antithesis will be swept away by the millennial Kingdom of God.

20:7   And when the thousand years shall be
finished, satan shall be loosed out of his prison, and
shall go forth and seduce the nations which are over
the four quarters of the earth, Gog, and Magog, and
shall gather them together to battle, whose number is
as the sand of the sea.

> *20:8   And they ascended upon the breadth of the
> earth, and surrounded the camp of the saints, and the
> beloved city.*
>
> *20::9   And fire came down from God out of heaven,
> and devoured them: and the devil, who seduced them,
> was cast into the pool of fire and brimstone, where
> both the beast*
>
> *20:10   And the false prophet shall be tormented day
> and night for ever and ever.*

At the conclusion of the Millennium, Satan is released from hell to tempt mankind once more, but fails again, this time for the last time, at the battle of Gog and Magog. This is the third great war of the Book of Revelation, the others being Babylon and Armagedon.

Even less is revealed about the Gog and Magog war than about the others. It may well be that like Armagedon, it will primarily be a conflict of supernatural and superhuman proportions. It is very likely that other prophets shall arise from those living in the Millennium to provide greater details and warnings. Evidently those living then will be exceptional saints, but still vulnerable to temptations. St. John assures us that the "devil who seduces them" will be cast into hell along with the Beast and False Prophet previously judged.

> *20:11   And I saw a great white throne, and him that
> sat upon it, from whose presence the earth and heaven
> fled away, and there was no place found for them.*
>
> *20:12   And I saw the dead, great and small,
> standing before the throne, and the books were
> opened: and another book was opened, which is
> the book of life: and the dead were judged by
> those things which were written in the books
> according to their works.*
>
> *20:13   And the sea gave up the dead that were in it:
> and death and hell gave up their dead that were in
> them: and they were judged every one according to
> their works.*
>
> *20:14   And hell and death were cast into the pool of
> fire. This is the second death.*
>
> *20:15   And whosoever was not found written in the
> book of life, was cast into the pool of fire.*

Now comes the great "white throne," the final judgment of mankind which we will all be called to. It's difficult to understand how Protestants can claim that we are saved by "faith alone" when it's clear from St. John that we will be judged by our works. Twice St. John says, of both those written in the book of life and also those cast into the lake of fire, "They were judged according to their works."

In the original text, only this last section, P-9, and the first, W-1, are in their correct chronological order. Many writers were at a disadvantage previously by not knowing the correct sequence and their resulting interpretations were necessarily skewed, although many have noted that St. John seemed to return to the same events over and over.

Did St. John scramble the order of Revelation or did the Holy Spirit guide his hand? Whatever the case, it was obviously not critical to unravel them until now when the time has come for people to actually live the events. I hope this reorganized text will help to serve as a guide and handbook as the end-time tragedies unfold and we all can begin to understand what to expect next.

WHO IS THE ANTICHRIST?

Many people wonder who will be the Antichrist, the dictator of the New World Tyranny. What is more amazing is that so many of our current so-called world leaders would be more than happy to sell their souls in order to gain this pinnacle of success. As it is, they will support him since he will need 12 false apostles in order to mimic Christ. But beware to you phony world leaders for your hero will destroy three of you and your countries as prophesied by Daniel and by our Lady of Fatima who called your destruction the "annihilation of nations."

If the Antichrist has a name, St. John avoids any reference to it, nor does he even use the term, "Antichrist." He always calls him the "Beast" and portrays him with animalistic features like the "mouth of a lion," the "feet of a bear," and the "look of a leopard." As we approach the days of this "man of dark secrets," it would be wise for us not to give him any recognition whatsoever.

Because St. John never refers to the Antichrist by name, some claim that the "Beast" is not one individual. Some also confuse the Antichrist Beast with the One World Beast. But only an individual can be cast into hell and St. John writes of both the Antichrist and the False Prophet, "These two were cast alive into the lake of fire." (Rev. 19:20) The author says these "two" because they are never more than numbers to him like the number 666 which St John assigns to the Man of Sin.

According to another theory, the Antichrist could be a woman. Is this the reason God will ask a Woman (Mary) to be His agent in defeating the Antichrist because it would be unseemly for Christ to conquer a woman? Also, in the divine trinity, Father, Son and Holy Spirit, the Holy Spirit represents the feminine and shouldn't there be a similar feminine person in the unholy trinity of Antichrist, False Prophet and Satan? Or could it be the False Prophet who is a woman, in other words, not an antipope but a female clergy person who leads the One World Religion?

To argue against any of these scenarios, it should be noted that all previous precursors to the Antichrist — Goliath, Haman, Nero, Henry VIII, Hitler, Stalin and many others — have been male. It seems pretty conclusive that it can only be Satan who exudes an unholy reflection of the Holy Spirit. Nor has it been unusual for Satan to appear before Saints as a temptress, a female test for their virtue. It really is a waste of time to try and guess the name of Antichrist. We will know soon enough and then we will wish we didn't know!

One of the more interesting prophecies about the Antichrist is that he will be able to change time and seasons. I believe this prophecy refers to the number relegated to him by God, 666. Since he cannot change his numerical designation, he will try anything to give importance and prominence to the number 6.

For example, he will try to change highway speed limits from 55 mph and 65 mph to 56 mph and, even better, 66 mph. He will also try to change currency from $5 bills, $10 bills or $50 bills to $6 bills or $66 bills. Since he will be ridiculed for such silly attempts, he will eliminate money altogether and enforce worldwide use of debit cards and ultimately implanted microchips, the "mark of the Beast."

I predict the Antichrist will have much greater success in altering times and seasons. First, he will eliminate the two twelve-hour segments of the day and substitute four 6-hour segments: morning, afternoon, evening, and early morning. Twelve months will also irritate him so he will create 6 months with 60 days each. The new months will be named after 6 seasons: winter, spring, planting, summer, fall, and harvest. Each new month will consist of ten 6-day weeks or perhaps 6 ten-day weeks. He may even reinstate the calendar of the French Revolution. Either way, Sunday will be eliminated.

In order to get a full year, the Antichrist will add a six-day festival, in his honor, of course, at the end of the six 60-day months. This will replace Christmas and New Years and he will abolish all other religious and national holidays as well. If you're lucky, he might give workers a six-day weekend following six consecutive six-day work weeks. Whatever the case, the Antichrist's goal will be for everyone's lives to revolve around his number, the number six, the number of imperfection, the number of the Beast.

Normally this kind of tinkering with time and season would be universally derided as folly, but the Antichrist will be particularly annoyed that our current Gregorian calendar was named after and promulgated by a Pope, Pope Gregory the Great.

Even after gaining full authority over the One World Tyranny, the Antichrist will find difficulty rearranging the calendar without support from organized religion. This is where the False Prophet, the Antipope of all time, comes in. He will betray his sacred office and give legitimacy to any and all foul plans of the Beast. Catholics, be forewarned! Whatever you do, you must not accept the mark of the Beast, despite what the False Pope may claim. Saving your soul will depend on it! You may be able to remember the Lord's Day even when everyone else is following six-day weeks, but the mark of the Beast will be permanent, irreversible and ultimately fatal.

Fortunately, the length of time the Antichrist reigns will be "shortened" as promised by Jesus. However, it may last much longer than the usually quoted time of three and one-half years. The period given in the bible for his term of office is "a time, two times and half a time" or 1260 days. Admittedly these add up to three and a half years, but they actually must be interpreted as symbolic numbers.

The number three and one half is significant, not as a specific length of time, but because it is one-half the perfect number of seven. In other words, the Antichrist may rule longer than three and one-half years, but whatever his length of rule, it will be one half the length of time normally expected. Thus his end will be premature, his days shortened. At the time of his rule, he will, of course, be well aware of the 1260 day prophecy, and he will mock Christians when he lasts longer. He will offer this as proof that he is a true messiah, not an antichrist. So be prepared for this setback and discouragement. His end will come soon enough, sooner that he expects.

The Antichrist's two main nemeses are Enoch and Elias. These witnesses thwart his plans at every turn and delay his public debut as the Antichrist. They prevent him from carrying out his fiendish "final solution" to the Christian problem. When the Antichrist succeeds in killing the Two Witnesses, he knows his pathway to success in "liquidating" all Christians is clear.

From the Book of Esther, we know that it is at this darkest moment for the elect that his time will be shortened as promised by Jesus. Through Mary's intercession, the chastising comet appears and at last the days will be numbered for the Antichrist and his One World Tyranny. The number may not be exactly 1260 days but the point is it will be much shorter than he would like.

The Antichrist's response to the appearance of the chastising comet is to gather the armies of the world for the Battle of Armagedon. Satan probably convinces him that he and his armies have the supernatural power it takes to defeat Almighty God! St. John provides no details of the Antichrist's defeat but simply says that he is taken and cast into Hell. As mentioned earlier, Christians must not be curious about how Jesus on his white horse and Raptured army win the battle. If we try to observe this scene of supernatural judgment, we will end up like Lot's wife who was turned into a pillar of salt when she dared to look back at God's destruction of Sodom and Gomorrah.

MYSTERY BABYLON

St. John sees the name written on the forehead of the harlot, but he doesn't recognize it because it is undoubtedly in a foreign language, so he calls the harlot "Babylon." The name that St. John sees but does not recognize is "Capitalism." Many other exegetes have interpreted different titles, systems or religions for the harlot's name, but none fit the prophecy better than "Capitalism." I will leave it to other exegetes to determine why the author refers to Babylon as a woman while the Beast she rides upon is masculine.

The destruction of the harlot (Capitalism) by the scarlet Beast that she rides (Communism) will be one of the most amazing events in world history. How can an inferior, third rate economic and political tyranny like Communism, which, by the way, has already "collapsed", overcome the economic, political and military might of Capitalism? This predicted event is also the most significant of all the tribulations documented in the Apocalypse simply in terms of the amount of space St. John devotes to describing this catastrophe.

The secret to discovering the Achilles heel which leads to the downfall of Capitalism lies in her name, "harlot." Capitalism is an amoral system. The Wall Street Journal has often been called the "Bible" of Capitalism, but you will never find this "Bible" taking a stand against pornography, fornication, adultery, divorce, homosexuality, or abortion. Pornography is a billion-dollar business and abortion takes the lives of 1.5 million babies every year just in America alone, but Capitalism merely counts these as successful enterprises. No wonder when Capitalism is destroyed we find these words in the Apocalypse: "Rejoice over her, you heaven, and you holy apostles and prophets; for God has judged your judgment on her." (18:20)

At the apparition site of Fatima, the Blessed Mother told the seers Lucy, Jacinta and Francisco that more people go to hell for sins of the flesh than any other sin. Whereas individuals are sent to hell for their transgressions, nations cannot undergo this type of judgment. Nations must pay for their crimes on this planet, not in hell, and history is replete with the fall of nations due to their moral decadence.

Another prime characteristic of Capitalism is her fantastic

economic capabilities. After her fall, the Socialist leaders of earth lament, even though they had approved of her demise, because they had gotten rich through trading with her. The Apocalypse is clear that greed and wealth is the second main reason God allows judgment on Capitalism. The "bottom line" is the "God" of Capitalism, and the Lord God permits no God besides Him! The third reason for Babylon's demise is her involvement with "sorceries" and "enchantments," in other words the occult.

Of course, the Capitalist countries will not possibly conceive how their defeat can come about and they will scoff at my suggestions in this book. As St. John poetically expresses it, they will say of themselves, "I sit a queen, and am no widow; and sorrow I shall not see." (18:7) But prophecy must be fulfilled and the next chapter describes the mighty Beast that does the harlot in.

THE SCARLET BEAST

The Scarlet Beast which the whore of Babylon (Capitalism) controls, represents Socialist/Communism. Six of the seven heads of the Beast represent past great tyrannical kingdoms while the seventh, and last, is this great One World Empire. The ten horns represent the nations of the world which have adopted Socialism or Communism to one degree or another, most of which will be derived from the ancient Roman Empire. Just as sexual sins are the hallmark of Capitalism, the great vice of the Beast is blasphemy. Atheism is a communist's personal perversion.

The eighth beast, which is "of the seventh," symbolizes the victorious, revived reign of One World Communism. The "inhabitants of the earth (whose names are not written in the book of life from the foundation of the world) shall wonder seeing the Beast that was and is not" and goes to destruction. The way God annihilates this last One World Communist Government will be even more spectacular than the one hour defeat of Capitalism. However, it will be forbidden for Christians to observe this spectacle.

If Capitalism seems indestructible, how much more difficult will it be to overthrow the New World Disorder? The Bible says this confederation of all the world's nations will have one purpose: the stamping out of all vestiges of Christianity. The people will say, "Who will be able to fight it?"

The end of the eighth Beast, the One World Tyranny, begins with the appearance of the chastising comet. "The angel took the censor, and filled it with fire of the altar, and cast it on earth, and there were thunders, and voices and lightnings and a great earthquake." (8:5; P-2)

All the people who have taken the mark and set up an idol of the beast are highly indignant at this turn of events. St. John reports, "The nations were angry, and your wrath is come, and the time of the dead, that they should be judged and that you should render reward to your servants, the prophets and the saints, and to them that fear your name, little and great, and destroy them who have polluted the earth." (11:18; P-4)

As the comet gets closer, the Antichrist undoubtedly believes he has the Satanic power to stop this punishment and he and the nations assemble their armies to fight the rider on the White Horse, not apostasy in this case, but Christ the Lamb and His Raptured saints, at the Battle of Armagedon. The Lord, of course, prevails and an angel instructs the birds of the air to feed on the carcasses of the "kings, horses, little and great" who fall from the fire of the comet and the sword of Jesus' mouth. The fate of the Scarlet Beast fulfills St. John's prophecy: "It goes to destruction." (17:11; W-9)

DANIEL'S VISIONS

The Old Testament prophet Daniel experiences several strange and powerful visions of the end times, its One World Tyranny and its leader, the Antichrist. The chief characteristics of this tyranny are very similar to those of St. John in the Apocalypse. As shown to Daniel, this last tyranny will be a successor to former world tyrannies and a confederation of ten nations. It will be more powerful than all previous governments put together. Its leader, the Antichrist, will be consummate evil himself, who can be defeated only by God's direct intervention.

Daniel's' first and most famous end times vision is in response to a dream which King Nebuchadnezzar had of a great and terrible statue made with a head of gold, chest of silver, belly of bronze, legs of iron and feet partly of iron and part clay. Daniel says to the king, "There is a God in heaven that reveals mysteries, who has shown you, O King Nebuchadnezzar, what is to pass in the latter times."

> *2:40*   *And the fourth kingdom shall be as iron. As iron breaks into pieces, and subdues all things, so shall that break and destroy all these.*

> *2:41*   *And whereas you saw the feet, and the toes, part of potter's clay, and part of iron: the kingdom shall be divided, but yet it shall take its origin from the iron, according as you saw the iron mixed with the miry clay.*

> *2:42   And as the toes of the feet were part of iron,*
> *and part of clay, the kingdom shall be partly strong,*
> *and partly broken.*

> *2:43   And whereas you saw the iron mixed with*
> *miry clay, they shall be mingled indeed together with*
> *the seed of man, but they shall not stick fast one to*
> *another, as iron cannot be mixed with clay."*

The part of Daniel's vision that most concerns us in the end times is the feet of iron and clay. The ten toes represent the nations led by the Antichrist which Daniel sees as a loose confederation consisting primarily of former states of the Roman Empire, the Kingdom of Iron. As we've noted before, since ten is a symbolic number signifying completion, the confederation actually consists of all the world's nations.

Some exegetes suggest that the clay refers to silica used in computer chips and the iron represents the numerous technological tools we use, including computers, which are integral to our civilization. Daniel's' reference to the "seed of man" included in the mix means that everyone will be required" to take the microchip mark of the beast in his hand or forehead during the reign of the New World Disorder.

This microchip in the body will make everyone a slave of the system, simply a cog in the machine. In this future totally materialistic society, a man or woman will be just one more scrap of fabric in the quilt. Current fads like body piercing, tattoos, face painting, microchips in animals, debit cards, etc., are being promoted to make it psychologically easier to accept a chip under the skin. As many others are warning today, we will be merely a number in the equation. But, as St. John warns, this is anathema to God, and those who accept the mark of the Beast will be cast ultimately into the lake of fire along with the Antichrist and the False Prophet. The "stone" cut out of the mountain (Dan. 2:45) is a clear indication that it is God who will end the One World Anti-system.

In Daniel's second vision, he sees four beasts come up out of the sea ("sea" in prophecy means "peoples"). The beasts are a lioness with wings, a bear with three rows of teeth, and a leopard with four wings. A fourth Beast, more terrifying than the others, has ten horns from which a smaller horn erupts which destroys three of the ten horns. The first three beasts are all reflected in St. John's description of the Beast from the sea (Antichrist) (13:2). The fourth "terrifying" Beast is the same as the seventh/eighth Communist Empire.

> *7:23   And thus he said: The fourth beast shall be*
> *the fourth kingdom upon earth which shall be greater*
> *than all the kingdoms, and shall devour the whole*
> *earth, and shall tread it down, and break it in pieces.*

> *7:24   And the ten horns of the same kingdom, shall*
> *be ten kings: and another shall rise up after them, and*
> *he shall be mightier than the former, and he shall*
> *bring down three kings.*
>
> *7:25   And he shall speak words against the High*
> *One, and shall crush the saints of the most high:*
> *and he shall think himself able to change times and*
> *laws, and they shall be delivered into his hands*
> *until a time, and times, and half a time.*

Here is yet another verification of the last One World Tyranny which consists of all nations, with the evil Antichrist as its leader, who will destroy several of them. As great as he and his kingdom is, it will be broken by divine judgment and given to the saints.

In Daniel's' third vision of the end times, he sees a struggle between a ram and a goat which eventually yields a little horn. The little horn is another portrait of the Antichrist, his evil and powerful nature, and his almost total success in destroying the Catholic Church.

> *8: 11   And it was magnified even to the prince of*
> *the strength: and it took away from him the continual*
> *sacrifice, and cast down the place of his sanctuary.*
>
> *8:12   And strength was given him against the*
> *continual sacrifice, because of sins: and truth shall be*
> *cast down on the ground, and he shall do and shall*
> *prosper.*
>
> ———
>
> *8:24   And his power shall be strengthened, but not*
> *by his own force: and he shall lay all things waste,*
> *and shall prosper, and do more than can be believed.*
> *And he shall destroy the mighty, and the people of the*
> *saints,*
>
> *8:25   According to his will, and craft shall be*
> *successful in his hand: and his heart shall be puffed*
> *up, and in the abundance of all things he shall kill*
> *many: and he shall rise up against the prince of*
> *princes, and shall be broken without hand.*

The continual sacrifice (8:11-13) which the Antichrist takes away is the Holy Sacrifice of the Mass. The "power" that strengthens him is Satan but in the end, when he tries to rise up against the "prince of princes" (Christ), he shall be "broken without hand," which is his supernatural defeat at Armagedon. Again, all these details about the end times fit exactly with the same events in the Apocalypse.

ISRAEL

One of the important signs that we are in the end times is the resurgence of the nation-state of Israel. Jesus said that this is how we would know we were in those days: "Now from the fig tree learn this parable, when its branch is now tender and the leaves break forth you know that summer is near, even at the door." (Mt. 24:32) In this oft-quoted passage, the fig tree is a symbol of Israel.

This does not mean that the modern state of Israel is the same as the people of Israel with whom God made His covenant. We must remember that Jesus also said that in the latter days, the Jews would accept the Antichrist as their Messiah. "I have come in the name of my Father, and you do not receive me. If another come in his own name, him you will receive." (Jn. 5:43) The Jews, like everyone else who takes the mark of the Beast, will suffer the same fate as the Antichrist and the Antipope.

In the Apocalypse, St. John enumerates 144,000 out of the twelve tribes of Israel who will be servants of God signed on their foreheads. The sign they will be marked with is the Sign of the Cross or, in the Hebrew alphabet, the letter TAU. After this group of saved Jews, St. John describes the gentiles who will be saved: "A great multitude, which no man could number, of all nations and tribes, and peoples and tongues." (Rev. 7:9, B-2)

Isn't it interesting that when St. John lists all those who "come out of the great tribulation and wash their robes and make them white in the blood of the Lamb," he mentions the Jews first. Even at the very end of days, the Jews are a chosen people, a nation set apart. The phrase "Jews for Jesus" is not a misnomer. Even when Jews accept Jesus as their Messiah, the still retain their Jewish heritage.

THE ROSARY AND CORRESPONDING SEGMENTS

A notable feature of the new text structure is the number five segments which merit further examination. W-5, R-5, B-5, and P-5 act as dividers or turning points between the first four and last four events in each phase of the end times: Apostasy, War, Tribulation, and Armagedon. The first four events are always announced by one of the four horsemen and the last four events which follow the pivotal number five segments are always announced by a herald angel.

The four number five events have a life of their own of great significance. They narrate a brief history of the Church as it reflects the life of Christ and also as Christ's life is depicted in the Rosary.

W-5, R-5, B-5 and P-5 mirror the Joyful, Luminous, Sorrowful, and Glorious Mysteries and also the birth, life, death and resurrection of the Church.

In W-5, the "woman" brings forth a "man child who was to rule all nations with an iron rod." The child is not only Christ, but also the Catholic Church which Mary gives birth to. This segment clearly expands on the Joyful Mysteries of the Rosary, particularly the nativity.

R-5 depicts five ways to defeat the devil, just as the Luminous Mysteries provide insights into some of the sacramental powers displayed during Christ's brief public ministry on earth. First, Satan loses his primordial battle with St. Michael. Next, the saints overcome him through the blood of the Lamb. Third, the woman manages to escape from his clutches, and fourth, the earth swallows up the flood which Satan sends after to drown her. Lastly, the Dragon goes to make war with the rest of the woman's spiritual children, a war he is destined to lose.

In the third segment, B-5, the Church is crucified just like her bridegroom, Jesus Christ. The key paragraph is 13:7 which tersely reveals the Antichrist's total subjugation of the Church. This event corresponds with the Sorrowful Mysteries, especially the death and burial of our Lord.

The last segment, P-5, describes the glorious resurrection of the Church, just as the Glorious mysteries tell of Christ's rebirth. 144,000 faithful and true Raptured Christians stand with Christ on Mt. Sion ready to begin the thousand-year Millennium on earth.

Just as the ROC chart reveals four dividing segments of the fifteen end time chapters which parallel the four mysteries of the Rosary, the entire Book of Revelation as a whole is similarly divided. The first three chapters consist of letters by St. John to seven churches in Asia which symbolize the fledgling church and therefore correspond to the early years of Christ's life on earth as expounded in the Joyful mysteries of the Rosary.

The next two chapters describe four fantastic creatures which worship at the throne of God plus an image of Christ holding the Scroll which He will unseal in the end times section. These chapters, four and five, correspond with the luminous mysteries of the Rosary which in turn chronicle Jesus' institution of the sacraments as well as His public ministry.

The next fifteen chapters, which we have already analyzed extensively, concern the passion of the Church, its trials, its sufferings and eventual martyrdom. Certainly these are a vivid reflection of the sorrowful mysteries of the Rosary.

Lastly, the "New Heaven and the New Earth," as delineated in the final two chapters, refer to the Church in Glory, just as the Glorious mysteries of the Rosary relate both Jesus' and Mary's Ascensions into Heaven. Thus St. John organizes his writing in such a way as to give honor to Mary's Rosary which is the ultimate weapon and our one hope for victory over the final wiles of Satan.

THE MARTYRED, THE RAPTURED, THE PROTECTED

There are eight sections where martyrs for the Lord are mentioned. The first four groups in W-2, W-7, R-5 and B-2 wear white robes, play harps, or indicate by some other means that they are in heaven and have already received their eternal reward. The Apostasy group (W-2) is told to wait until "their fellow servants are to be slain." The martyrs in W-7 are killed during the preliminary stage of the reign of the Antichrist and in R-5 more martyrs occupy heaven who "overcame Satan through the blood of the Lamb." Finally, in B-2, the last martyrs before the full reign of the Antichrist, 144,000 Jews and a multitude of Gentiles, earn their crowns during the Great Tribulation.

In B-6, however, just following St. John's description of the Two Beasts and therefore the beginning of the full reign of the Antichrist, the situation changes. Now the martyrs are referred to as "blessed" and from "henceforth" they rest from their labors. The word "henceforth" means that those who are martyred from now until the very end at Armagedon will enjoy a special privilege: they will return to earth with Christ and reign with Him during the Millennium.

These martyrs are described later in P-9 as the "souls that are beheaded." In B-6 they are described as the "dead" and they have three characteristics: they "die in the Lord," they "rest from their labors," and their "works follow them." In P-9, these same "souls" are given seven more attributes: they are "beheaded," they "testify for Jesus," they "testify for God," they do not "adore the beast," nor his "image," nor take the mark on their "foreheads," nor on their "hands." As we will discover, these Martyred, like the Raptured and the Protected, evince a total of ten attributes.

Several more succeeding groups are also described in different terms than those who were martyred previously. In B-9, a "great multitude" is also "blessed" because they are "called to the marriage supper of the Lamb (Millennium)". This is a strong contrast to the earlier martyrs who wear white, play harps, and are obviously in heaven. These are the Raptured who also do not suffer martyrdom and seem to dwell (temporarily) in a heavenly place, although probably not paradise itself. Very likely they are in the same spiritual plateau where the Two Witnesses, Enoch and Elias, wait for their return to earth. They constitute the great army which will "follow" Christ to earth.

As the Raptured wait "near" heaven for their return with Christ onto Mt. Sion (P-5), they are designated "singing servants" who sing with three traits: the "voice of a great multitude," the "voice of many waters," and the "voice of many thunders." In section P-5, we meet the exact same group which we should recognize as the Raptured saints who return to earth because they sing their "new canticle" with almost the exact same adjectives: the "noise of many waters," the "voice of great thunder," and the "voice of harpers." To these traits are added seven more: "undefiled with women," "virgins," "followers of the Lamb," "purchased from among men," "first fruits to God and the Lamb," "without lie," and "without spot".

In this passage the act of rapture is called "purchasing." This is an important phrase because St. John mentions it twice: these Raptured are "purchased from the earth" and "purchased from among men." Incidentally, this is a good verification from the author that when he uses the symbol "earth" he intends it to mean "mankind ."

In section B-8 we meet a third "blessed" group, but they exhibit only two attributes: they "watch" and they "keep their garments." This is very unusual because St. John hardly ever uses two descriptions when he can use three. This group appears again in P-9 and they attain three more traits: they are given "seats," they "sit on the seats" and they receive "judgment." Here St. John could easily make two descriptions do for three since receiving "seats" and "sitting on them" is almost identical phraseology. The author obviously separated them on purpose because he wanted these Protected to have a total of five attributes. So where are the other five? The Protected need five more traits to match the total of ten ascribed to the Martyred and the Raptured!

To find the missing five, we need to return to section R-5 where Mary's "seed" (spiritual children) flee into the desert. As we have noted, the "Woman" represents Mary as well as her faithful children. Their five additional attributes include: they are "persecuted," they receive "wings," they "flee into the desert," they receive "nourishment," and they are "helped by the earth". A combination of seven and three characteristics, as with the Raptured and Martyred would not work here because the number five is required to manifest Mary's Rosary.

All three millennial groups ultimately display a total of ten characteristics and the three groups together constitute a "solid, liquid, gas" trinity. The Beheaded suffer what is termed a "wet" martyrdom because of the extensive bloodletting. The Protected flee to a dry desert place while the Raptured complete the trinity since they are taken up in the air. The word "blessed" is the term St. John applies to all three millennial groups and he refers to them a total of seven times in the end time chapters.

It is the new text revisions of the ROC chart which clarify the status of all three groups of faithful Christians and martyrs throughout the Apocalypse. In the original sequence, for example, the 144,000 Raptured who return with Christ on Mt. Sion were described back in Chapter 14 **before** the martyrs in Chapter 15 who play their harps in heaven and sing the canticle of Moses. But St. John writes that the 144,000 Raptured sing a **new** canticle. It's only when we rearrange the text into its true chronological order that we find the Raptured group, who sings their **new** canticle, **after** the earlier martyred group in heaven, which do **not** return to earth and sings the **old** canticle of Moses.

NUMEROLOGY IN REVELATION

Whole books have been written on the spiritual significance of numbers (numerology), especially as used by apocalyptic prophets like Daniel and St. John. The most commonly used numbers in Revelation are 2, 3, 4 and 7. Larger numbers are almost always combinations of these particular digits. The author rarely uses 5, 6, 9 or higher which is a good indication that he uses the former numbers on purpose.

Section R-9, which details the destruction of Babylon (Capitalism), is chock full of significant numbers, although often not in their usual meaning. The number "2", for example, normally refers to mankind (a man and a woman). Here in R-9, St. John consistently employs a dual repetition of expressions as reference to the double land and sea assaults of WWIII. Occasionally, St. John will also use "2" to indicate two opposing or antagonistic entities or viewpoints.

The number "3", of course, expresses the Holy Trinity and three repetitions of the same event or expression provides a conclusive or "divine" emphasis. For instance, the word "holy" is important, but the phrase "holy, holy, holy" is more than just triply significant — it is "divinely" imperative!

The number "4" usually means all humanity (two couples) or universality (four winds from four directions, four seasons, etc.). In this section, however, St. John uses "4" as another way to express the Trinity because most of the quadruple events consist of three identical or similar occurrences plus one which is somewhat different or a generalized expression of the other three. This type of "4" can be seen in the four Gospels wherein St. John renders quite a different treatment of the same subject matter from that of Saints Matthew, Mark and Luke. Four, in this case, symbolizes the trinity as three persons in one God. This type of trinity (4) added to the more common trinity (3) equals 7, another number which expresses perfection and therefore the Divine.

Practically every paragraph in section R-9 lists at least one numerical significance:

18:1	(2) Heaven vs earth
18:2	(2) "is fallen, is fallen" (Babylon's two-fold destruction)
18:2	(3) Devils, unclean spirits, hateful birds
18:3	(3) Nations, kings, merchants
18:4	(2) avoid "sins" or receive "plagues"
18:5	(2+2) Lord and heaven vs sins and iniquity
18:6	(2+3) Babylon's dual destruction with a triple emphasis.
18:7	(2+2) glory and delicacies vs torment and sorrow
18:7	(3) Babylon's pride: queen, not widow, no sorrow
18:8	(4) Babylon's plagues: death, mourning, famine plus fire
18:9	(3+2) fornication & delicacies, weep & bewail, smoke & burning
18:10	(3+2) "alas, alas" (also in 18:16 and 18:19)
18:10	(3) "one hour" (also in 18:17 and 18:19)
18:11	(3) merchants + kings (18:9) + seamen (18:17)
18:12	(4) gold, silver, precious stones plus pearls
18:12	(4) purple, silk, scarlet plus fine linen
18:12	(3) thyine wood, ivory, stone vessels
18:12	(3) brass, iron, marble
18:13	(4) cinnamon, ointment, frankincense plus odors
18:13	(4) wine, oil, fine flour plus wheat
18:13	(3) beasts, sheep, horses
18:13	(3) chariots, slaves, souls of men
18:14	(3) fruits of desire, fat things, goodly things
18:15	(3) torments, weeping, mourning
18:16	(3) linen, purple, scarlet
18:16	(3) gold, precious stones, pearls
18:17	(4) shipmasters, sailors, mariners plus sea workers
18:18	(2+3) stood and cried plus seeing, burning, saying
18:19	(2+3) cast and cried plus weeping, mourning, saying

18:20	(3) heavens, apostles, prophets
18:22	(4) harpers, pipers, trumpeters plus musicians
18:23	(4) mill sound, lamp light, married voice plus craftsmen
18:23	(3) merchants, enchantments, blood
18:24	(3) prophets, saints, slain
19:1	(3) salvation, power, glory
19:1	(3) "alleluia," 19:3 "alleluia," 19:4 "alleluia"

R-9 is truly a gold mine of permutations and combinations which, I'm sure contain many more than I have uncovered. I doubt if you will ever find a more remarkable display of numerical virtuosity in all of literature. One of the reasons St. John warns translators and analysts not to add to or subtract from his work is because that would scramble his intricate numerology. I suspect that someone who understands the author's numerology could translate the original Greek and find many more examples. St. John put tremendous effort into composing this passage for one important reason: so that in these latter days no none would underestimate the coming catastrophe of the demise of Capitalism.

36 ANGELS

Another very important example of significant numbers in the fifteen end-times chapters is the appearance of 36 angels (not counting the many unnamed angels in Michael's army or demons in Satan's army.) St. John chooses the number 36 in order to precisely verify the ROC arrangement which divides these chapters into 36 subdivisions.

The 36 angels are separated into 9 individual groupings which in turn serve to substantiate the 9 passages on the ROC chart which follow the four horsemen. Thus there are 7 "trumpet" angels, 7 "bowl" angels, and 3 groups of 4 angels: 4 "Euphrates" angels, 4 "wind" angels and 4 "herald" angels. In addition, there are 3 groups of 3 angels each: 3 "sun" angels (B-2, B-4, P-9), 3 "altar" angels (B-7, P-2, P-9) and 3 "heaven" angels (R-9, P-6, P-9). And, finally there is one angel in his own group, St. Michael. Once again, the author is telling us that we must break down his work into 36 sections with 9 sections following each of the four horsemen if we are to comprehend his prophecies. St. John's numerology is not accidental!

Many commentators believe there is one more angel, the one like "the son of man" who sits on a cloud and reaps earth with a sharp sickle (P-6). Since this personage takes orders from another angel, he cannot be Christ. Besides, he is described "like" the son of man, not the Lord Himself. So the question is, why did St. John clearly indicate that this figure must be an angel, and yet obviously and purposely decline to describe him as an angel? Because, very simply, that would increase the number of identified angels to 37. Thus the author makes an emphatic point that he chooses 36 angels in 9 groupings deliberately in order to verify the unraveling of Revelation as it is presented on the ROC chart.

THE THIRD COMING OF CHRIST

Most people are familiar with the "second coming" of Christ although many confuse it with the not so well-known "third" coming of Christ. In the final two chapters of Revelation, St. John describes this third reign of the Lord, also known as the Parousia. These three advents of Christ, like so many other trinities in St. John's work, reflect the basic trinity of the universe around us: land, sea and air.

Jesus' first coming can very well be considered his "water" advent. From His conception in the watery womb of His mother Mary, to His bloody crucifixion, Jesus was surrounded by a liquid milieu. As noted earlier, Jesus' first miracle turned water into wine and His last miracle turned wine into His own blood. Between the two miracles some of his most unforgettable signs were fluidic in nature: walking on water, calming the storm at sea, choosing fishermen as His disciples, conversing with the woman at the well and preaching from a boat to people on shore. He even cured a blind man with spittle and mud.

Therefore, it's no surprise that Jesus' symbol is the fish. When He had to pay a tax, He instructed his apostles to catch a fish and they found the coin in its mouth. He referred to his greatest sign, His resurrection, as the sign of Jonah. Every aspect of his execution was wet and bloody from his sweating blood in the Garden of Gethsemane to His scourging and crowning of thorns, to the final lance in his side from which gushed blood and water.

Jesus second coming is his "land" advent and is described briefly in section P-5 when He stands on Mt. Sion with the 144,000 Raptured elect who return with Him to set up the millennial Kingdom. It's apparent that His "land" return begins on a mountain top far from any sea or body of water. St. John provides few details of what this reign will be like except that Jesus will rule with an iron rod although perhaps not iron willed enough because Satan will once again be allowed to tempt mankind near the end of the thousand years just before the final judgment. Many twentieth century seers who have been shown images of what life will be like on our planet after WWIII and the chastising comet describe a very barren, dry landscape.

The third advent of Christ completes the trilogy of His Kingdoms which St. John calls a "New Heaven and a New Earth" and which is definitely of an "air" or spiritual nature. There is specifically no sun and this "New" Jerusalem cannot possibly be located on planet earth. Jesus' third kingdom can only refer to paradise or as St. Paul says: "The third heaven" where he heard "secret words which it is not granted to man to utter." (II Cor. 12:2-4) Probably very few of us will attain to the second kingdom of Christ, the Millennium, but we all can look forward to the New Jerusalem if only we continue our walk with the Lord.

WHEN DOES THE FUTURE HAPPEN?

When discussing St. John's Book of Revelation and the end times, people invariably ask, "When are these things going to happen?" The Apostles asked Jesus the same question and He replied, "Of that day or hour no one knows, neither the angels nor the Son, but the Father only." (Mk.13-32) Obviously, if you really need to know, you must ask the Father!

Jesus said that it would come upon us suddenly: "Watch therefore for you know neither the day nor the hour." (Mt. 24-22) But He also added that we should learn to read the signs: "When you see all these things coming to pass, know that it is near, even at the door." (Mt. 13-29) Therefore we must not act like the five foolish virgins or "despise prophecy" (1 Thess. 5-20) if we wish to "take care that no one leads us astray." (Mt. 24-4)

One day, during the Pontificate of Pope Leo XIII, he overheard a locution between God and the Devil. God agreed to give Satan 100 years to mount a final attack against humanity. The Pope immediately composed a prayer to St. Michael which used to be recited after all Catholic Masses (a requirement which our Bishops in their "wisdom" have since abrogated.) If the 100 years began in 1917 with the appearances of our Blessed Mother at Fatima and the Bolshevik revolution, then the 100 years is up in 2017. This date coincides with the conclusion of the "five months" (centuries) since Martin Luther posted his 95 theses.

If the seven year tribulation period precedes 2017 rather than after, and if WWIII occurs before that, then we are certainly very close. Of course, there are a lot of "ifs" in that sentence! Since we cannot and should not live our lives based on "ifs" the only true answer is: be ready at all times. We know that the signs which Jesus gave us — wars, rumors of wars, earthquakes in diverse places, persecutions of the faithful — are already here. If we are unprepared we will, like the five foolish virgins, lose out on the greatest banquet of all time, the "marriage feast of the Lamb."

IN CONCLUSION

It's amazing but true that the correct chronological sequence of the third section of the Book of Revelation has been overlooked until now. Past commentators have always remained somewhat mystified as to its juggled order and hidden content. As H. M. Feret wrote, "The numerous literary conventions employed by the inspired writer — septenaries and dove-tailings, antitheses and recapitulations, parallelism and anticipations, etc., and their various combinations — make it very difficult to establish with certainty any detailed plan of his book." [10]

Rearranging the text according to the simple plan on the ROC chart, clears up these problems concerning order, content and meaning, which the Holy Spirit evidently wanted to be kept secret until the very end of days. Ven. Anne Catherine Emmerich prophesied that toward the end of time, there would arise several men who would unlock the mysteries of the Apocalypse. This book fulfills that promise.

It must be noted that although the entire text has been totally restructured, every word and phrase as well as all poetic images and descriptions are positively intact (see appendix A). It may seem incongruous for the sixth angel to blow his trumpet (Huge Army, R-4) before the third angel blows his trumpet (Wormwood, B-3) but the new time sequence is correct because the "Huge Army" occurs during World War III while the fallen star "Wormwood" occurs later during the Great Tribulation. It might be easier to visualize if we use a sports analogy and see the angels with team number on their "jerseys." There is no sport where the players score in the same sequence as the numerals on their backs!

Still, it is very important that St. John numbered his visions in the original because they serve to mark the separation point of one event from another. Only eight of the thirty-six events on the chart are not so numbered — W-5, R-5, B-5, P-5 and W-9, R-9, B-9, P-9 — and it proves to be fairly easy to find the breaking points for those passages so that they fit into the established pattern.

Restructuring also separates and consolidates the passages

---

[10] Feret, H. M. The Apocalypse Explained, p. 227.

which refer to the three wars. Section W-9 and all of the "R" sections, except R-5, cover the first war, World War III, Babylon vs the Beast. Four more sections, B-8, B-9, P-6, and P-9 describe the second war, Armagedon, the Beast vs the Lord. The third war, which occurs at the end of the Millennium, Gog and Magog vs the Lamb, is mentioned briefly only once in P-9.

In summary, St. John's powerful warnings seem to be directed chiefly at us lay people rather that at the clergy, and are of a two-fold nature. First, for those of you living under Capitalism (Babylon), do not partake of her crimes: luxury, occultism and abortion. Instead, you must "go out from her" if you wish to "avoid her plagues."

Second, if you live under the One World Tyranny, which will soon be all of us, do not take the "mark of the beast" (microchip), or worship his image, but neither can you take up arms against this evil system. As Jesus said, "He who would save his life will lose it, he who would lose his life for my names sake will find it." (Mt. 16:25) My personal advice is: live your life so perfectly that you could qualify to be Protected or Raptured, but don't run and hide from the fact that like the Jesus you love, you may suffer the pains of martyrdom.

P.S. - EXTRAPOLATION

Sometimes St. John does not connect all the dots between his visions and the reader must extrapolate in order to get the complete picture. For example, the three groups which fight with the Lamb against the Antichrist are the "called, and elect, and faithful." (17:14) These three undoubtedly are the "raptured", the "protected" and the "beheaded" respectively. But only the "called" and the "faithful" have those specific words applied to them: "Blessed are the dead who die in the Lord" because they "keep the **faith** of Jesus" (14:12-13) and "Blessed are they that are **called** to the marriage supper of the Lamb." (19:9)

The "elect" who also fight in the Lamb's army, which can be extrapolated by the process of elimination, must be the "protected". Although the word "elect" is never applied to them it is clear they are "elected" by God to go with Mary to her place of protection in the desert. It's also very possible that at some point in the original Greek text St. John did use the word "elect" but that it was lost in the translation.

Another example is the possible connection between the "kings from the rising of the sun" who cross the Euphrates and invade the West during WWIII and the three wild beasts which express the Antichrist: the bear, lion and leopard. The only obvious link is that the "horses" of the invading armies have "heads of lions" (9:17) and the Antichrist has a "mouth of a lion." (13:2) The Antichrist is also depicted with the "feet of a bear" which probably indicates that Russia is one of the invading armies and the lion and leopard may point to China and Iran. Again, it's possible that these extrapolations would become much clearer from a more exact translation. On the other hand, a more careful study of the Greek may indicate that there is no connection.

In addition, I claim another extrapolation for myself personally, namely the designation of "Apocalypse Eagle":

"And I heard the voice of one eagle flying through
the midst of heaven, crying with a loud voice: Woe,
woe, woe to the inhabitants of the earth." (8:13)

The first "eagle" was St. Vincent Ferrer (1350-1419) who warned people in many European countries about the impending break-up of Christianity (the first woe). He passed his "eagle" mantle to St. Bernardino of Siena (1380-1444) who continued his mission. St. Bernardino often warned his listeners that they were about to receive the "plague of locusts" which we now understand to be symbols of Martin Luther and his followers.

When St. John uses the term "one eagle" he implies that there are more than one. That the first two "eagles" preached only about the first "woe" also indicates more than one "eagle". As the "third eagle" my goal is to try and prevent the devastating effects of WWIII, the second "woe", as much as possible. Following my commission, there will come a fourth "eagle" who will warn about the reign of Antichrist and the last "woe", the Great Chastisement and the battle of Armagedon. Thus from St. John's term "one eagle", plus the historicity of St. Vincent Ferrer and St. Bernardino, we can extrapolate the last two "eagles" whose missions are to reveal the final "woes" on mankind.

APPENDIX A:
BOOK OF REVELATION, CHAPTERS 6-20

W1 6:1 And I saw
That the Lamb had opened one of the seven seals:
And I heard one of the four living creatures
As it were the voice of thunder, saying:
Come, and see.

6:2 And I saw:
And behold a white horse,
And he that sat on him had a bow,
And there was a crown given him.
And he went forth conquering, that he might conquer.

W2 6:9 And when he had opened the fifth seal,
I saw under the altar the souls of them that were slain for the
word of God,
And for the testimony which they held.

6:10 And they cried with a loud voice, saying:
How long, O Lord (holy and true)
Do you not judge and avenge our blood
On them that dwell on earth?

6:11 And white robes were given to every one of them.
And it was said to them, that they should rest for a little time,
Till their fellow servants , and their brethren,
Who are to be slain, even as they,
Should be filled up.

W3 8:6 And the seven angels, who had the seven trumpets,
Prepared themselves to sound the trumpet.

8:7 And the first angel sounded the trumpet,
And there followed hail and fire, mingled with blood:
And it was cast on the earth. And the third part of the earth
was burnt up.
And the third part of the trees was burnt up.
And all green grass was burnt up.

W4 8:13   And I beheld:
And heard the voice of one eagle flying through
the midst of heaven,
Crying with a loud voice: Woe, woe, woe to the
inhabitants of the earth
By reason of the rest of the voices of the three angels,
Who are yet to sound the trumpet.

9:1   And the fifth angel sounded the trumpet,
And I saw a star fall from heaven upon the earth.
And there was given to him the key of the bottomless pit.

9:2   And he opened the bottomless pit:
And the smoke of the pit arose, as the smoke
of a great furnace.
And the sun and the air were darkened with the smoke
of the pit.

9:3   And from the smoke of the pit there came out locusts
upon the earth.
And power was given to them as the scorpions
of the earth have power,

9:4   And it was commanded them that they should not hurt
The grass of the earth, nor any green thing or any tree,
But only the men who have not the sign of God upon their
foreheads.

9:5   And it was given unto them that they should not kill them,
But that they should torment them, five months.
And their torment was as the torment of a scorpion when it
strikes a man.

9:6   And in those days, man shall seek death, and shall not find it.
And they shall desire to die, and death shall fly from them.

9:7   And the shapes of the locusts
Were like unto horses prepared unto battle,
And on their heads were, as it were, crowns like gold;
And their faces were as the faces of men.

9:8   And they had hair as the hair of women:
And their teeth were as lions:

9:9   And they had breastplates as breastplates of iron:
And the noise of their wings was as the noise of chariots
And many horses running to battle.

9:10 And they had tails like to scorpions, and there were stings in
their tails;
And their power was to hurt men, five months,
And they had over them

9:11 A king, the angel of the bottomless pit,
Whose name in Hebrew is Abaddon, and in Greek Apollyon,
in Latin Exterminans.

9:12   One woe is past;
And behold, there come yet two woes more hereafter.

W5   12:1   And there appeared a great sign in heaven:
A woman clothed with the sun,
And the moon under her feet,
And on her head a crown of twelve stars.

12:2   And she being with child, cried travailing in birth:
And was in pain to be delivered.

12:3   And there appeared another sign in heaven.
And behold a great red dragon,
Having seven heads and ten horns,
And on his heads seven diadems.

12:4   And his tail drew the third part of the stars of heaven
And cast them to the earth.

And the dragon stood before the woman
Who was ready to be delivered:
That, when she should be delivered,
He might devour her son.

12:5   And she brought forth a man child
Who was to rule all nations with an iron rod.
And her son was taken up to God and to his throne.

12:6   And the woman fled into the wilderness,
Where she had a place prepared by God,
That there they should feed her a thousand two hundred and
sixty days.

W6   14:6   And I saw another angel flying through the midst of heaven,
Having the eternal gospel, to preach unto them that sit upon
the earth,
And over every nation, and tribe, and tongue, and people:

14:7   Saying with a loud voice:
Fear the Lord, and give him honor,
Because the hour of his judgment is come.
And adore you him, that made heaven and earth,
The sea, and the fountains of water.

W7   15:1   And I saw another sign in heaven, great and wonderful:
Seven angels having the seven last plagues.
For in them is filled up the wrath of God.

15:2   And I saw as it were a sea of glass mingled with fire:
And them that had overcome the beast and his image
And the number of his name,
Standing on the sea of glass,
Having the harps of God:

15:3 And singing the canticle of Moses, the servant of God,
And the canticle of the Lamb, saying:
Great and wonderful are your works, O Lord God Almighty.
Just and true are your ways, O King of ages.

15:4 Who shall not fear you, O Lord, and magnify your name?
For you only art holy.
For all nations shall come and shall adore in your sight
Because your judgments are manifest.

15:5 And after these things, I looked:
And behold the Temple of the tabernacle
of the testimony in heaven
Was opened.

15:6 And the seven angels came out of the temple,
having the seven plagues,
Clothed with clean and white linen,
And girt about the breasts with golden girdles.

15:7 And one of the four living creatures gave
to the seven angels seven golden bowls
Full of the wrath of God, who lives for ever and ever.

15:8 And the temple was filled with smoke
From the majesty of God, and from his power.

And no man was able to enter into the temple
Till the seven plagues of the seven angels were fulfilled.

16:1 And I heard a great voice out of the temple, saying to the
seven angels:
Go and pour out
The seven bowls of the wrath of God upon the earth.

16:2 And the first went and poured out his bowl upon the earth,
And there fell a sore and grievous wound
Upon men who had the character of the beast:
And upon them that adored the image thereof.

W8 16:10 And the fifth angel poured out his bowl
Upon the seat of the beast;
And his kingdom became dark,
And they gnawed their tongues for pain.

16:11 And they blasphemed the God of heaven,
Because of their pains and wounds,
And did not penance for their works.

W9 17:1 And there came one of the seven angels,
who had the seven bowls,
And spoke with me, saying:
Come, I will show you the condemnation of the great harlot
Who sits upon many waters.

17:2   With whom the kings of the earth have
        committed fornication
        And they who inhabit the earth
        Have been made drunk with the wine of her prostitution.

17:3   And he took me away in the spirit into the desert.
        And I saw a woman sitting upon a scarlet colored beast,
        Full of names of blasphemy,
        Having seven heads and ten horns.

17:4   And the woman
        Was clothed round in purple and scarlet,
        And gilded with gold and precious stones and pearls,
        Having a golden cup in her hand,
        Full of the abomination and filthiness of her fornication.

17:5   And on her forehead a name was written:
        A mystery:
        Babylon the great, the mother of the fornications and
        abominations of the earth.

17:6   And I saw the woman drunk with the blood of the saints,
        And with the blood of the martyrs of Jesus.
        And when I had seen her, I wondered with great admiration.

17:7   And the angel said to me:
        Why do you wonder?
        I will tell you the mystery of the woman,
        And of the beast which carries her,
        Which has the seven heads and ten horns.

17:8   The beast which you saw, was, and is not,
        And shall come up out of the bottomless pit
        And go into destruction:
        And the inhabitants of the earth

        (Whose names are not written in the book of life
        from the foundation of the world)
        Shall wonder,
        Seeing the beast that was and is not.

17:9   And here is the understanding that has wisdom.
        The seven heads are seven mountains, upon
        which the woman sits,
        And they are seven kings.

17:10   Five are fallen, one is, and the other is not yet come;
        And when he shall come, he must remain a short time.

17:11   And the beast that was and is not:
        The same is also the eighth, and is of the seven,
        And goes into destruction.

17:12   And the ten horns, which you saw, are ten kings
        Who have not yet received a kingdom,
        But shall receive power as kings
        One hour after the beast.

17:13 These have one design,
And their strength and power they shall deliver to the beast.

17:14 These shall fight with the Lamb,
And the Lamb shall overcome them;
Because he is Lord of lords, and King of kings;

And they that are with him
Are called, and elect, and faithful.

17:15 And he said to me:
The waters which you saw
Where the harlot sits,
Are peoples, and nations, and tongues.

17:16 And the ten horns, which you saw on the beast,
These shall hate the harlot,
And shall make her desolate and naked,
And shall eat her flesh, and shall burn her with fire.

17:17 For God has given into their hearts to do
that which pleases him:
That they give their kingdom to the beast
Till the words of God be fulfilled.

17:18 And the woman which you saw,
Is the great city, a kingdom which has dominion
over the kings of the earth.

R1 6:3   And when he had opened the second seal,
I heard the second living creature, saying:
Come and see.

6:4   And there went out another horse that was red:
And to him that sat thereon, it was given
That he should take peace from the earth,
And that they should kill one another,
And a great sword was given to him.

R2 6:12   And I saw,
When he had opened the sixth seal,
And behold there was a great earthquake,
And the sun became black as sackcloth of hair:
And the whole moon became as blood.

6:13   And the stars from heaven fell upon the earth,
As the fig tree casts its green figs
When it is shaken by a great wind:

6:14   And the heaven departed as a scroll when it is rolled together:
And every mountain and the islands were moved out
of their places.

6:15   And the kings of the earth, and the princes, and tribunes,
And the rich and the strong,
And every bondsman and every freeman hid
themselves in the dens
And in the rocks of mountains.

6:16   And they say to the mountains and the rocks:
Fall on us, and hide us
From the face of him that sits upon the throne
And from the wrath of the Lamb:

6:17   For the great day of their wrath is come,
And who shall be able to stand?

R3   8:8   And the second angel sounded the trumpet:
And as it were a great mountain, burning with fire,
was cast into the sea,
And the third part of the sea became blood.

8:9   And the third part of those creatures died which
had life in the sea,
And the third part of the ships was destroyed.

R4   9:13   And the sixth angel sounded the trumpet:
And I heard a voice from the four horns of the golden altar
Which is before the eyes of God,

9:14   Saying to the sixth angel who had the trumpet:
Loose the four angels, who are bound
In the great river Euphrates.

9:15   And the four angels were loosed,
Who were prepared for an hour, and a day, and a month, and
a year,
For to kill the third part of men.

9:16   And the number of the army of the horsemen was
Twenty thousand times ten thousand.
And I heard the number of them.

9:17   And thus I saw the horses in the vision,
And they that sat on them had breastplates of fire and of
hyacinth and brimstone.
And the heads of the horses were as the heads of lions;
And from their mouths proceeded fire, and smoke, and
brimstone.

9:18   And by these three plagues was slain the third part of men,
By the fire and by the smoke and by the brimstone
Which issued out of their mouths.

9:19   For the power of the horses is in their mouths,
and in their tails.
For their tails are like to serpents, and have heads;
And with them they hurt.

9:20   And the rest of the men, who were not slain by these plagues,
Did not do penance from the works of their hands,
That they should not adore devils and idols of gold and
silver and brass,
And stone and wood,
Which neither can see nor hear nor walk.

9:21   Neither did they penance from their murders,
        Nor from their fornications, nor from their thefts.

R5   12:7   And there was a great battle in heaven:
        Michael and his angels fought with the dragon,
        And the dragon fought, and his angels.

12:8   And they prevailed not,
        Neither was their place found any more in heaven.

12:9   And that great dragon was cast out, the old serpent,
        Who is called the devil and Satan,
        Who seduces the whole world.
        And he was cast forth unto the earth,
        And his angels were thrown down with him.

12:10   And I heard a loud voice in heaven, saying:
        Now is come salvation, and strength,
        And the kingdom of our God, and the power of his Christ:
        Because the accuser of our brethren is cast forth,
        Who accused them before our God day and night.

12:11   And they overcame him by the blood of the Lamb,
        And by the word of their testimony,
        And they loved not their lives unto death.

12:12   Therefore rejoice, O you heavens, and you that dwell therein.
        Woe to the earth, and to the sea,
        Because the devil is come down unto you, having great wrath,
        Knowing that he has but a short time.

12:13   And after the dragon saw that he was cast unto the earth,
        He persecuted the woman who brought forth the man child.

12:14   And there were given to the woman two wings
        of a great eagle,
        That she might fly into the desert to her place,
        Where she is nourished for a time, and times,
        and half a time,
        From the face of the serpent.

12:15   And the serpent cast out of his mouth, after the woman,
        Water, as it were a river;
        That he might cause her to be carried away by the river.

12:16   And the earth helped the woman,
        And the earth opened her mouth
        And swallowed up the river
        Which the dragon cast out of his mouth.

12:17   And the dragon was angry against the woman:
        And went to make war with the rest of her seed,
        Which keep the commandments of God
        And have the testimony of Jesus Christ.

12:18   And he stood upon the sand of the sea.

R6   14:8   And another angel followed, saying:
That great Babylon is fallen, is fallen;
Which made all nations to drink
Of the wine of the wrath of her fornication.

R7   16:3   And the second angel poured out his bowl upon the sea,
And there came blood as it were of a dead man;
And every living soul died in the sea.

R8   16:12   And the sixth angel poured out his bowl
upon that great river Euphrates
And dried up the water thereof,
That a way might be prepared for the kings
From the rising of the sun.

R9   18:1   And after these things
I saw another angel coming down from heaven,
Having great power:
And the earth was enlightened with his glory.

18:2   And he cried out with a strong voice, saying:
Babylon the great is fallen, is fallen:
And is become the habitation of devils,
And the hold of every unclean spirit,
And the hold of every unclean and hateful bird.

18:3   Because all nations have drunk of the wine
of the wrath of her fornication
And the kings of the earth have committed fornication
with her;
And the merchants of the earth have been made
rich by the abundance of her delicacies.

18:4   And I heard another voice from heaven, saying:
Go out from her, my people:
That you be not partakers of her sins,
And that you receive not of her plagues.

18:5   For her sins have reached even to heaven,
And the Lord has remembered her iniquities.

18:6   Render to her as she also has rendered to you:
And double unto her double according to her works:
In the cup, wherein she has mingled,
Mingle unto her double.

18:7   As much as she has glorified herself,
and has lived in delicacies,
So much torment and sorrow give you to her.
Because she says in her heart: I sit a queen,
and am not a widow:
And sorrow I shall not see.

18:8 Therefore shall her plagues come in one day,
Death, and mourning, and famine,
And she shall be burnt with fire,
Because God is strong, who shall judge her.

18:9 And the kings of the earth, who have committed fornication,
And lived in delicacies with her,
Shall weep, and bewail themselves over her,
When they shall see the smoke of her burning.

18:10 Standing afar off for fear of her torments,
Saying: Woe! woe! that great city, Babylon,
that mighty city:
For in one hour is your judgment come.

18:11 And the merchants of the earth shall weep
and mourn over her:
For no man shall buy their merchandise any more:

18:12 Merchandise of gold, and silver, and of precious stones,
And pearls, and of fine linen, and purple,
and of silk, and scarlet,
And all thyine wood, and all manner of vessels of ivory,
And all manner of vessels of precious stone,
And of brass, and iron, and marble,

18:13 And cinnamon and of odors and ointment, and frankincense,
And wine, and oil, and fine flour, and wheat,
And beasts, and sheep and horses, and chariots,
And slaves, and souls of men.

18:14 And the fruits of the desire of your soul
are departed from you,
And all fat and goodly things are perished from you,
And they shall no more find them.

18:15 The merchants of these things, who were made rich,
Shall stand afar off from her, for fear of her torments,
Weeping and mourning

18:16 And saying: Woe! woe! that great city,
Which was clothed with fine linen, and purple, and scarlet,
And was gilded with gold, and precious stones, and pearls:

18:17 For in one hour are so great riches come to naught.
And every shipmaster,
And every one that sails into the lake, and mariners,
And they that work at sea,
Stood afar off,

18:18 And cried out, seeing the place of her burning, saying:
What city is like to this great city?

18:19 And they cast dust upon their heads, and cried out,
Weeping and mourning, saying: Woe! woe! that great city,
Wherein all were made rich, who had ships at sea,
by reason of her prices:
For in one hour she is made desolate.

18:20 Rejoice over her, you heaven,
And you holy apostles, and prophets:
For God has judged your judgment on her.

18:21 And a mighty angel took up a stone,
As it were a great millstone,
And cast it into the sea, saying:
With this violence shall Babylon, that great city,
Be thrown down, and shall now be found no more.

18:22 And the voice of harpers, and of musicians,
And of them that play on the pipe, and on the trumpet,
Shall no more be heard in you:
And no craftsman of any art whatsoever shall be
found any more in you:
And the sound of a mill shall be heard no more in you.

18:23 And the light of a lamp
Shall shine no more in you;
And the voice of the bridegroom and bride
Shall be heard no more in you.
For your merchants were the great men of the earth,
For all nations have been deceived by your sorceries.

18:24 And in her has been found the blood of prophets and of saints
And of all who were slain upon the earth.

19:1 After these things
I heard as it were the voice of many multitudes in heaven,
Saying:
Alleluia. Salvation, and glory, and power is to our God:

19:2 For true and just are his judgments, who has judged
the great harlot,
Which corrupted the earth with her fornication,
And has revenged the blood of his servants, at her hands.

19:3 And again they said:
Alleluia.
And her smoke ascends for ever and ever.

19:4 And the four and twenty ancients, and the four living
creatures,
Fell down and adored God, that sits upon the throne,
Saying: Amen. Alleluia.

B1 6:5 And when he had opened the third seal,
I heard the third living creature saying:
Come and see. And behold a black horse,
And he that sat on him had a pair of scales in his hand.

6:6 And I heard as it were a voice in the midst
of the four living creatures,
Saying: Two pounds of wheat for a penny,
And thrice two pounds of barley for a penny,
And see you hurt not the wine and the oil.

B2 7:1 After these things I saw four angels
Standing on the four corners of the earth,
Holding the four winds of the earth,
That they should not blow upon the earth,
Nor upon the sea, nor on any tree.

7:2 And I saw another angel ascending from
the rising of the sun,
Having the seal of the living God.
And he cried with a loud voice to the four angels
To whom it was given to hurt the earth and the sea:

7:3 Saying: Hurt not the earth, nor the sea, nor the trees,
Till we seal the servants of our God in their foreheads.

7:4 And I heard the number of them that were sealed,
A hundred forty-four thousand sealed,
Of all the tribes of the children of Israel.

7:5 Of the tribe of Juda, twelve thousand sealed:
Of the tribe of Ruben, twelve thousand sealed:
Of the tribe of Gad, twelve thousand sealed:

7:6 Of the tribe of Aser, twelve thousand sealed:
Of the tribe of Naphtali, twelve thousand sealed:
Of the tribe of Manasses, twelve thousand sealed:

7:7 Of the tribe of Simeon, twelve thousand sealed:
Of the tribe of Levi, twelve thousand sealed:
Of the tribe of Issachar, twelve thousand sealed.

7:8 Of the tribe of Zabulon, twelve thousand sealed:
Of the tribe of Joseph, twelve thousand sealed:
Of the tribe of Benjamin, twelve thousand sealed.

7:9 After this I saw a great multitude,
Which no man could number,
Of all nations, and tribes, and peoples, and tongues,
Standing before the throne, and in the sight of the Lamb,
Clothed with white robes,
And palms in their hands:

7:10 And they cried with a loud voice, saying:
Salvation to our God, who sits upon the throne,
And to the Lamb.

7:11 And all the angels stood round about the throne,
And about the ancients, and about the four living creatures.
And they fell before the throne upon their faces,
And adored God,

7:12 Saying: Amen.
      Benediction and glory, and wisdom, and thanksgiving,
      Honor, and power, and strength to our God
      For ever and ever. Amen.

7:13 And one of the ancients answered and said to me:
      Who are these that are clothed in white robes,
      and whence are they come?

7:14 And I said to him: My lord, you know.
      And he said to me: These are they who are come out
      of great tribulation,
      And have washed their robes, and have made them white
      In the blood of the Lamb.

7:15 Therefore they are before the throne of God,
      And serve him day and night in his temple.
      And he that sits on the throne shall dwell over them.

7:16 They shall not hunger nor thirst any more,
      Neither shall the sun fall on them, nor any heat.

7:17 For the Lamb, which is in the midst of the throne,
      shall rule them,
      And shall lead them to the fountains of the waters of life,
      And God shall wipe away all tears from their eyes.

B3 8:10 And the third angel sounded the trumpet:
      And a great star fell from heaven, burning as it were a torch.
      And it fell on the third part of the rivers
      And upon the fountains of waters:

8:11 And the name of the star is called Wormwood.
      And the third part of the waters became wormwood;
      And many men died of the waters,
      Because they were made bitter.

B4 10:1 And I saw another mighty angel
      Come down from heaven clothed with a cloud.
      And a rainbow upon his head,
      And his face was as the sun, and his feet as pillars of fire:

10:2 And he had in his hand a little scroll, open:
      And he set his right foot upon the sea,
      And his left foot upon the land:

10:3 And he cried out with a loud voice, as when a lion roars.
      And when he had cried out, seven thunders uttered their
      voices.

10:4 And when the seven thunders had uttered their voices,
      I was about to write.
      And I heard a voice from heaven saying to me:
      Seal up the things which the seven thunders have spoken
      And write them not.

10:5 And the angel, which I saw standing upon the sea,
and upon the land,
Lifted up his hand to heaven:

10:6 And he swore by him that lives for ever and ever,
Who created heaven, and the things which are therein;
And the earth, and the things which are therein;
And the sea, and the things which are therein:
That there shall be no more delay:

10:7 But that in the days of the voice of the seventh angel,
When he shall begin to sound the trumpet,
The mystery of God shall be finished,
As he has declared by his servants, the prophets.

10:8 And I heard a voice from heaven
Speaking to me again, and saying:
Go, and take the scroll, that is open,
From the hand of the angel standing
Upon the sea and upon the land.

10:9 And I went to the angel, saying unto him,
That he should give me the scroll.
And he said to me: Take the scroll and devour it:
And it shall make your belly bitter,
But in your mouth it shall be sweet as honey.

10:10 And I took the scroll from the hand of the angel,
And devoured it:
And it was in my mouth sweet as honey:
And when I had devoured it, my belly was bitter:

10:11 And he said to me:
You must prophesy again to nations, and peoples, and
tongues, and to many kings.

11:1 And there was given me a reed like unto a rod,
And it was said to me:
Rise, and measure the temple of God,
And the altar,
And them that adore in it.

11:2 But the court, which is without the temple,
Cast out, and measure it not,
Because it is given to the Gentiles,
And the holy city they shall tread under foot forty-two
months:

11:3 And I will give to my two witnesses,
And they shall prophesy a thousand two hundred sixty days,
Clothed in sackcloth.

11:4 These are the two olive-trees, and the two candlesticks,
standing before the Lord of the earth.

11:5   And if any man would hurt them,
       Fire shall come out of their mouths, and shall
       devour their enemies.
       And if any man would hurt them,
       In this manner must he be killed.

11:6   These have power to shut heaven,
       That it rain not in the days of their prophecy:
       And they have power over waters
       To turn them into blood
       And to strike the earth with all plagues
       As often as they will.

11:7   And when they shall have finished their testimony,
       The beast that ascends out of the abyss
       Shall make war against them and shall overcome
       them and kill them.

11:8   And their bodies shall lie in the streets of the great city,
       Which spiritually is called Sodom and Egypt:
       Where also their Lord was crucified.

11:9   And they of the tribes, and peoples, and tongues, and nations,
       Shall see their bodies for three days and a half:
       And shall not suffer their bodies to be laid in sepulchers.

11:10 And the inhabitants of the earth
       Shall rejoice over them, and make merry:
       And shall send presents one to another,
       Because these two prophets
       Tormented them that dwelled upon the earth.

11:11 And after three days and a half,
       The spirit of life from God entered into them.
       And they stood upon their feet,
       And great fear fell upon them that saw them.

11:12 And they heard a great voice from heaven saying to them:
       Come up hither.
       And they went up into heaven in a cloud: and their enemies
       saw them.

11:13 And at that hour there was a great earthquake,
       And the tenth part of the city fell.
       And there were slain in the earthquake, names
       of men seven thousand;
       And the rest were cast into a fear, and gave glory
       to the God of heaven.

11:14 The second woe is past: and behold the third woe
       will come quickly.

B5 13:1   And I saw a beast coming out of the sea,
       Having seven heads and ten horns;
       And upon his horns ten diadems,
       And upon his heads names of blasphemy.

13:2 And the beast which I saw was like to a leopard,
And his feet were as the feet of a bear,
And his mouth as the mouth of a lion.
And the dragon gave him his own strength
And great power.

13:3 And I saw one of his heads as it were wounded to death:
And his deadly wound was healed.
And all the earth was in admiration after the beast.

13:4 And they adored the dragon, which gave power to the beast.
And they adored the beast, saying:
Who is like to the beast?
And who shall be able to fight with it?

13:5 And there was given to it a mouth,
Speaking great things, and blasphemies:
And power was given to it to act
Forty-two months.

13:6 And he opened his mouth in blasphemies against God,
To blaspheme his name, and his tabernacle,
And them that dwell in heaven.

13:7 And it was given to him to make war with the saints,
And to overcome them.

And power was given him over every tribe, and people, and
tongue, and nation.

13:8 And all that dwell upon the earth adored him,
Whose names are not written in the book of life of the Lamb
Which was slain from the beginning of the world.

13:9 If any man have an ear, let him hear.

13:10 He that shall lead into captivity, shall go into captivity.
He that shall kill by the sword, must be killed by the sword.
Here is the patience and the faith of the saints.

13:11 And I saw another beast coming up out of the earth,
And he had two horns, like to a lamb's,
And he spoke as a dragon.

13:12 And he executed all the power of the former beast
in his sight:
And he caused the earth, and them that dwell therein,
To adore the first beast, whose deadly wound was healed.

13:13 And he did great signs,
So that he made even fire to come down from heaven
Upon the earth in the sight of man.

13:14 And he seduced them that dwell on the earth,
By the signs, which were given him to perform
in the sight of the beast,
Saying to them that dwell on the earth,

That they should make an image to the beast
Which had the wound by the sword and lived.

13:15 And it was given him to give life to the image of the beast,
And that the image of the beast should speak:
And should cause that whoever will not adore the
image of the beast
Should be slain.

13:16 And he shall make all, both little and great, rich and poor,
Freemen and bondmen,
To have a mark in their right hand or in their foreheads.

13:17 And that no man might buy or sell, but he that has the mark,
Or the name of the beast, or the number of his name.

13:18 Here is wisdom. He that has understanding, let him
Compute the number of the beast.
For it is the number of a man:
And his number is six hundred sixty-six.

B6   14:9   And the third angel followed them, saying with a loud voice:
If any man shall adore the beast and his image,
And receive his mark in his forehead, or in his hand;

14:10 He also shall drink of the wine of the wrath of God,
Which is mingled with pure wine in the cup of his wrath,
And shall be tormented with fire and brimstone
In the sight of the holy angels and in the sight of the Lamb.

14:11 And the smoke of their torments shall ascend up
for ever and ever:
Neither have they rest day nor night,
Who have adored the beast, and his image,
And whoever receives the mark of his name.

14:12 Here is the patience of the saints,
Who keep the commandments of God and the faith of Jesus.

14:13 And I heard a voice from heaven, saying to me:
Write:
Blessed are the dead who die in the Lord.
From henceforth now, said the spirit,
That they may rest from their labors,
For their works follow them.

B7   16:4   And the third poured out his bowl
Upon the rivers and the fountains of waters;
And there was made blood.

16:5   And I heard the angel of the waters saying:
You are just, O Lord,
Who are, and who was, the Holy One,
Because you have judged these things:

16:6   For they have shed the blood of the saints and prophets,
And you have given them blood to drink;
For they are worthy.

16:7   And I heard another, from the altar, saying:
Yes, O Lord God Almighty,
True and just are your judgments.

B8   16:13   And I saw from the mouth of the dragon,
And from the mouth of the beast, and from
the mouth of the false prophet,
Three unclean spirits like frogs.

16:14   For they are the spirits of devils working signs,
And they go forth unto the kings of the whole earth,
To gather them to battle against the great day
of Almighty God.

16:16   And he shall gather them together
Into a place which in Hebrew is called Armagedon.

16:15   Behold, I come as a thief.
Blessed is he that watches, and keeps his garments,
Lest he walk naked and they see his shame.

B9   19:5   And a voice came out from the throne, saying:
Praise you our God all his servants:
And you that fear him, little and great.

19:6   And I heard as it were the voice of a great multitude,
And as the voice of many waters,
and as the voice of great thunders,
Saying:
Alleluia: for the Lord our God, the omnipotent,
has reigned.

19:7   Let us be glad and rejoice: and give glory to him:
For the marriage of the Lamb is come,
And his wife has prepared herself.

19:8   And to her it has been granted, that she should clothe
herself with fine linen,
Glittering and white.
For the fine linen are the justifications of saints.

19:9   And he said to me: Write:
Blessed are they who are called to the marriage
supper of the Lamb.
And he said to me:
These words of God are true.

19:10   And I fell down before his feet, to adore him,
And he said to me: See you do it not.
I am your fellow-servant, and of your brethren

Who have the testimony of Jesus.
Adore God.
For the testimony of Jesus is the spirit of prophecy.

19:11 And I saw heaven opened, and behold a white horse.
And he that sat upon him was called Faithful and True,
And with justice he judges and fights.

19:12 And his eyes were as a flame of fire,
And on his head many diadems,
Having a name written,
Which no man knows but himself.

19:13 And he was clothed with a garment sprinkled with blood:
And his name is called: THE WORD OF GOD.

19:14 And the armies which are in heaven
Followed him on white horses,
Clothed in fine linen, white and clean.

19:15 And out of his mouth proceeds
A sharp two-edged sword:
That with it he may strike the Gentiles.
And he shall rule them with a rod of iron:
And he treads the wine press
Of the fury of the wrath of God the Almighty.

19:16 And he has on his garment and on his thigh written:
King of kings, and Lord of lords.

P1   6:7   And when he had opened the fourth seal,
I heard the voice of the fourth living creature saying:
Come, and see.

6:8   And behold a pale horse, and he that sat upon him,
His name was Death. And hell followed him.
And power was given to him over the four parts of the earth,
To kill with sword, with famine, and with death,
And with the beasts of the earth.

P2   8:1   And when he had opened the seventh seal,
There was silence in heaven,
As it were for half an hour.

8:2   And I saw seven angels standing in the presence of God;
And there were given to them seven trumpets.

8:3   And another angel came and stood before the altar,
Having a golden censer;
And there was given to him much incense,
That he should offer
Of the prayers of all saints
Upon the golden altar, which is before the throne of God.

8:4   And the smoke of the incense of the prayers of the saints
Ascended up before God from the hand of the angel.

8:5   And the angel took the censer
        And filled it with fire of the altar, and cast it on the earth,
        And there were thunders and voices and lightnings,
        and a great earthquake.

P3 8:12   And the fourth angel sounded the trumpet,
        And the third part of the sun was smitten,
        And the third part of the moon,
        And the third part of the stars,
        So that the third part of them was darkened.
        And the day did not shine for a third part of it,
        and the night in like manner.

P4 11:15   And the seventh angel sounded the trumpet;
        And there were great voices in heaven,
        Saying:
        The kingdom of this world is become our Lord's
        and his Christ's,
        And he shall reign for ever and ever. Amen.

        11:16   And the four and twenty ancients,
        Who sit on their seats in the sight of God
        Fell on their faces and adored God, saying:

        11:17   We give you thanks, O Lord God Almighty,
        Who are, and who was, and who is to come:
        Because you have taken to yourself great power,
        And you have reigned.

        11:18   And the nations were angry,
        And your wrath is come,
        And the time of the dead, that they should be judged,
        And that you should render reward to your servants
        the prophets,
        And the saints,
        And to them that fear your name, little and great,
        And should destroy them who have corrupted the earth.

        11:19   And the temple of God was opened in heaven;
        And the ark of his testament was seen in his temple.
        And there were lightnings, and voices, and an earthquake,
        and great hail.

P5 14:1   And I saw:
        And behold a Lamb stood on Mount Sion,
        And with him a hundred forty-four thousand
        Having his name, and the name of his Father,
        written in their foreheads.

        14:2   And I heard a voice from heaven, as the voice
        of many waters,
        And as the voice of great thunder:
        And the voice which I heard, was as of harpers,
        harping on their harps.

14:3   And they sung as it were a new canticle,
Before the throne, and before the four living creatures,
and the ancients: \
And no man could say the canticle
But those hundred forty-four thousand
Who were purchased from the earth.

14:4   These are they who were not defiled with women:
For they are virgins.
These follow the Lamb wherever he goes.
These were purchased from among men,
The first fruits to God, and to the Lamb:

14:5   And in their mouth was found no lie:
For they are without spot before the throne of God.

P6   14:14   And I saw:
And behold a white cloud:
And upon the cloud one sitting like to the Son of man,
Having on his head a golden crown,
And in his hand a sharp sickle.

14:15   And another angel came out of the temple,
Crying with a loud voice to him that sat upon the cloud:
Thrust in your sickle, and reap, because the hour
Is come to reap. For the harvest of the earth is ripe.

14:16   And he that sat on the cloud, put his sickle to the earth,
And the earth was reaped.

14:17   And another angel came out of the temple,
which is in heaven,
He also having a sharp sickle.

14:18   And another angel came out from the altar,
Who had power over fire:
And he cried with a loud voice to him that had the sharp
sickle, saying:
Thrust in your sharp sickle, and gather the clusters of the
vineyard of the earth:
Because the grapes thereof are ripe.

14:19   And the angel put his sharp sickle to the earth,
And gathered the vineyard of the earth
And cast it into the great press of the wrath of God.

14:20   And the press was trodden without the city:
And the blood came out of the press,
Up to the horses bridles,
For a thousand and six hundred furlongs.

P7   16:8   And the fourth angel poured out his bowl upon the sun,
And it was given to him
To afflict men with heat and fire:

16:9   And men were scorched with great heat:
And they blasphemed the name of God,
Who has power over these plagues.
Neither did they penance to give him glory.

P8   16:17   And the seventh angel poured out his bowl into the air,
And a great voice came out of the temple from the throne,
saying:
It is done.

16:18   And there were lightnings, and voices, and thunders,
And there was a great earthquake,
Such as never has been
Since men were upon the earth:
Such an earthquake, so great.

16:19   And the great city was made into three parts:
And the cities of the Gentiles fell,
And great Babylon came in remembrance before God,
To give to her the cup
Of the wine of the indignation of his wrath.

16:20   And every island fled away,
And the mountains were not found.

16:21   And great hail, like a talent,

Came down from heaven upon men:
And men blasphemed God for the plague of the hail
Because it was exceedingly great.

P9   19:17   And I saw an angel standing in the sun:
And he cried with a loud voice,
Saying to all the birds that did fly through
the midst of heaven:
Come, and gather yourselves together
to the great supper of God,

19:18   That you may eat the flesh of kings,
and the flesh of tribunes,
And the flesh of mighty men,
And the flesh of horses, and of them that sit on them,
And the flesh of all freemen, and bondmen,
and of little and great.

19:19   And I saw the beast,
And the kings of the earth and their armies
Gathered together to make war with him
That sat upon the horse and with his army.

19:20 And the beast was taken,
      And with him the false prophet,
      Who wrought signs before him, wherewith he seduced
      Them who received the mark of the beast
      and who adored his image.
      These two were cast alive into the pool of fire
      Burning with brimstone.

19:21 And the rest were slain by the sword of him
      that sits upon the horse,
      Which proceeds out of his mouth;
      And all the birds were filled with their flesh.

20:1 And I saw an angel coming down from heaven,
      Having the key of the bottomless pit
      And a great chain in his hand.

20:2 And he laid hold on the dragon, the old serpent,
      Which is the devil and Satan,
      And bound him for a thousand years:

20:3 And he cast him into the bottomless pit, and shut him up,
      And set a seal upon him,
      That he should no more seduce the nations
      Till the thousand years be finished. And after that,
      He must be loosed a little time.

20:4 And I saw seats. And they sat upon them:
      And judgment was given unto them.
      And the souls of them that were beheaded
      For the testimony of Jesus, and for the word of God,
      And who had not adored the beast, nor his image,
      Nor received his mark in their foreheads, or in their hands,
      And they lived and reigned with Christ a thousand years.

20:5 The rest of the dead lived not
      Till the thousand years were finished.
      This is the first resurrection.

20:6 Blessed and holy is he that has part in the first resurrection:
      In these the second death has no power.
      But they shall be priests of God and of Christ,
      And shall reign with him a thousand years.

20:7 And when the thousand years shall be finished,
      Satan shall be loosed out of his prison
      And shall go forth and seduce the nations
      Which are over the four quarters of the earth,
      Gog and Magog,
      And shall gather them together to battle,
      Whose number is as the sand of the sea.

20:8 And they ascended upon the breadth of the earth,
      And surrounded the camp of the saints, and the beloved city.

20::9 And fire came down from God out of heaven,
       And devoured them:
       And the devil, who seduced them,
       Was cast into the pool of fire and brimstone,
       Where both the beast

20:10 And the false prophet shall be tormented
       Day and night for ever and ever.

20:11 And I saw a great white throne,
       And him that sat upon it,
       From whose presence the earth and heaven fled away,
       And there was no place found for them.

20:12 And I saw the dead, great and small,
       Standing before the throne.
       And the books were opened, and another book was opened,
       Which is the book of life.
       And the dead were judged by those things
       which were written
       In the books according to their works.

20:13 And the sea gave up the dead that were in it:
       And death and hell gave up their dead that were in them.
       And they were judged, every one according to their works.

20:14 And hell and death were cast into the pool of fire.
       This is the second death.

20:15 And whosoever was not found written in the book of life
       Was cast into the pool of fire.

APPENDIX B:
THIRD SECRET OF FATIMA

Sister Lucia speaks, "After the two parts which I have already explained, at the left of Our Lady and a little above, we saw an Angel with a flaming sword in his left hand: flashing, it gave out flames that looked as though they would set the world on fire; but they died out in contact with the splendour that Our Lady radiated towards him from her right hand: pointing to the earth with his right hand, the Angel cried out in a loud voice: 'Penance, Penance, Penance!' And we saw in an immense light that is God: 'something similar to how people appear in a mirror when they pass in front of it' a Bishop dressed in White 'we had the impression that it was the Holy Father'. Other Bishops, Priests, men and women Religious going up a steep mountain, at the top of which there was a big Cross of rough-hewn trunks as of a cork-tree with the bark; before reaching there the Holy Father passed through a big city half in ruins and half trembling with halting step, afflicted with pain and sorrow, he prayed for the souls of the corpses he met on his way; having reached the top of the mountain, on his knees at the foot of the big Cross he was killed by a group of soldiers who fired bullets and arrows at him, and in the same way there died one after another the other Bishops, Priests, men and women Religious, and various lay people of different ranks and positions. Beneath the two arms of the Cross there were two Angels, each with a crystal aspersorium in his hand, in which they gathered up the blood of the Martyrs and with it sprinkled the souls that were making their way to God."

---

[1]Kramer, Paul, Rev., compiler and editor. *The Devil's Final Battle: How the Current Rejection of the Message of Fatima Causes the Present Crisis in the Church and the World*, p. 98.

APPENDIX C:
BIBLIOGRAPHY

Feret, H. M. *The Apocalypse Explained*. Fort Collins, CO: Roman Catholic Books, 1958.

Gallery, Rev. John Ireland. *Mary vs Lucifer: The Apparitions of Our Lady*, 1531-1933. Milwaukee: Bruce Publishing Co., 1960.

Holy Bible. Douay-Rheims Version.

Kramer, Rev. Herman Bernard. *The Book of Destiny*. Rockford, IL: Tan Books and Publishers, Inc., 1955.

Kramer, Rev. Paul, compiler and editor. *The Devil's Final Battle: How the Current Rejection of the Message of Fatima Causes the Present Crisis in the Church and the World*. Terryville, CT: The Missionary Association, 2002.

Martindale, C. C., S.J. *Saint John and the Apocalypse*. Fort Collins, CO: Roman Catholic Books, 1922.

Marystone, Cyril. *The Shepherds Are Lost*.

Our Lady of the Roses, Mary Help of Mothers Shrine (Bayside Prophecies).

Pelletier, Joseph A. *Our Lady Comes to Garabandal*. Worcester, MA: An Assumption Publication, 1971.

Prophecies of St. Malachy. Rockford, IL: Tan Books and Publishers, Inc.